Quilted
forest décor

Terrie Kralik

©2005 Terrie Kralik
Published by

kp krause publications
An Imprint of F+W Publications

700 East State Street • Iola, WI 54990-0001
715-445-2214 • 888-457-2873

Our toll-free number to place an order or obtain a free catalog is (800) 258-0929.

Photos on the following pages were taken by Terrie Kralik: 2, 3, 4, 5, 6.

Library of Congress Catalog Number: 2005922942
ISBN-13: 978-0-87349-952-1
ISBN-10: 0-87349-952-2
Edited by Susan Sliwicki
Designed by Donna Mummery

Printed in the United States of America

Dedication

My family has supported, encouraged and inspired me. Thank you from the bottom of my heart! I dedicate this book to you.

Acknowledgments

My sincere thanks to the people with whom I've worked at the following companies and businesses: Bernina of America, M.C.G. Textiles, P&B Textiles, Sulky of America, Timber Lane Press and The Warm Company. A special thanks goes to Golden Eagle Log Homes for letting us photograph projects in their beautiful homes.

Contents

You Are Invited

To: Talk about quilts in the forest.

Where: Your backyard, a neighborhood park or nature area.

When: Your next day off, about 10 a.m.

Why: Please accept this invitation to join me in the forest, enjoying a few quiet moments for inspiration with me. No RSVP needed... See you there!

Introduction

I'm excited to share some quilting thoughts with you. First, sit down at your picnic table or on a quilt in the shade of a tree. Bring a glass of iced tea or lemonade, take a deep breath, and relax.

Now, let's talk about quilts.

Between the covers of this book, you will find shy animals that only show their faces after they get to know you as friend instead of foe. Picture yourself in the woods beside me, looking at these magnificent animals, and you'll be able to see the potential of each design. Look for inspiration as you glance at these forest animals in their natural surroundings. Some projects focus on the animal, but are mostly pieced; others have minimal piecing and focus on a scene.

For anglers, have fun with the variety of fishing designs included. Add your own silhouette to the Fish Tale Wall Hanging, or incorporate your child's first fish into another project, such as the Fish-In-A-Round Wall Hanging. Hunters and outdoor enthusiasts will love the numerous choices of quilts with game animals. Photographers and hikers will appreciate how realistic and detailed the animals are, and they may recognize some of the scenes or hoof prints. Interior designers will be thrilled with the coordinating accessories.

The projects are grouped by subject — Fin, Fur, Feather and Flora — but many of the motifs are interchangeable. Some instructions include special notes that give hints or tricks specific to a pattern. Sew matching items for your home, such as wall hangings, table runners, place mats, coasters and napkins. Feel free to improvise and add your favorite animals or designs to what I've provided. Or, combine projects into your own work. This is your part of the forest, so go ahead and decorate it to fit your lifestyle.

At the start of this book, you'll find a reference section that covers terminology, tools and techniques, such as using fusible web. Fusibles continue to be an important element in my projects, so I've explained several ways to finish the raw edges, plus alternatives for those who prefer other methods over fusibles.

Speed piecing techniques are used often in these projects, so look for a section devoted to them, fully describing how to make certain pieced units. My thorough instructions make a great reference guide for novice and experienced quilters alike. Once you master these processes, you'll be able to use them with all of your piecing!

In my own quilting, I like to understand how a designer approaches fabric selection, color and piecing. For that reason, I've included everything from color tips to measuring for borders, as well as a variety of quilting designs and finishing instructions. You also will find a glossary of terms on page 127.

Tips are placed strategically throughout the book to help you avoid mistakes that I have made or to provide general information learned from experience. I hope that you find these tidbits valuable.

If you hope to recreate a project exactly as shown, you may be disappointed, as many fabrics will be discontinued by the time this book is released. Time moves on, and fabric goes out the door, into your stash or mine. Look for something similar in design and color to what appealed to you, and you will be just as successful with your project. Your local quilt shop will be your best resource as you search for the perfect fabrics from current fabric lines.

Finally, I challenge you to enjoy your quilting. Enjoy the process of selecting your project and the steps you go through to bring it to life. Feel the joy and satisfaction that comes with completing your first project. Every time you look at that project, you'll get to step back into the peaceful beauty of the forest.

But now it's time for both of us to get back to the sewing room. Happy quilting!

Terrie.

LAYOUT DIAGRAM

Chapter 1
Getting Started

Tools

Tools for quilters constantly are being reinvented and improved, so be sure to check your local quilt shop for the latest and greatest items that are available.

Treat yourself to the best tools and equipment; it will make the process of quilting easier and more enjoyable. For best results, start with a sewing machine that has been freshly serviced and fitted with a brand-new needle. And yes, rotary cutters, rulers and mats do wear out, so replace them.

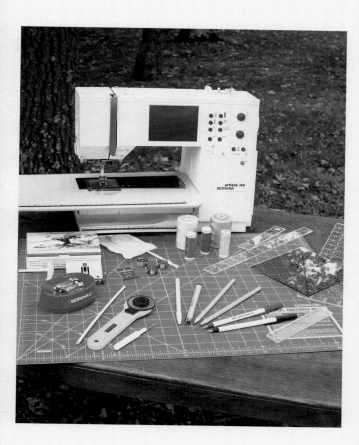

Here is a list of basic tools and supplies that you will need to complete the projects in this book:

Sewing
- Sewing machine
- Walking foot (to piece and quilt; I use this foot for almost everything)
- ¼" foot (optional; to piece; many quilters prefer this foot)
- Zipper foot (to complete pillow cording)
- Darning foot (to free-motion machine quilt)
- Straight-stitch throat plate (optional)
- Extra bobbins
- Extra size 80/12 sewing machine needles

General Notions
- 100 percent cotton thread in neutral colors for piecing in other colors to coordinate with projects
- Assorted decorative and specialty threads in different weights and textures to match and contrast designs as needed (see Contributors)
- Glass-head straight pins
- Magnetic pincushion
- Seam ripper
- Stylus or bamboo chopstick
- Measuring tape
- Temporary spray adhesive (to baste small projects)
- 1" safety pins (to baste larger projects)

Marking Tools
- No. 2 pencil
- Mechanical pencil
- White chalk pencil
- Green and red colored pencils (optional)

Cutting Equipment and Rulers
- Dressmaker scissors (to cut large appliqués)
- Embroidery scissors (to cut detailed and small appliqués)
- Small scissors (to cut threads at the machine)
- 45 mm rotary cutter with a new blade
- 12" x 18" and 18" x 24" cutting mats
- 1" x 6", 6" x 12" and 6" x 24" rulers
- 12½" or 15" square ruler
- 6" bias square ruler

Appliqué Supplies
- Iron
- Firm ironing board
- Pressing cloth
- Nonstick pressing sheet
- Freezer paper
- Paper or tear-away stabilizer
- Tweezers
- Black permanent marking pen (like Pigma Micron 05 or 03)

Tips and Techniques

Sewing Tips

- Sewing machine maintenance is vital. Frequently clean, oil and remove lint from your machine. Take your machine to a professional for regular servicing.
- Use the throat plate designed for the task at hand. Not all machines have more than one option, but for those that do, make sure you pick the right throat plate.
- Replace needles often. Bent or dull needles can affect stitch quality. If you can't recall when you last changed your needle, it's time now!
- Use the correct size of sewing machine needle for the job (usually a size 80/12).
- Set your machine to stop with the needle in the down position, if you have that option.
- Sew with an accurate ¼" seam. Double check your seam width often as you work, and make adjustments to your stitching as needed. Keep a 1" x 6" ruler beside your sewing machine for this purpose.
- Chain sew as much as possible for speed and accuracy. Chain sewing is stitching one seam right after another, without cutting the threads between pieces. By repeatedly sewing the same pieces together, you will notice quickly when something is out of line.
- Use a stylus to help guide fabric through the sewing machine. It's especially helpful when sewing over bulky seams and at intersections.
- Be aware of the trade-offs of speed sewing techniques. They are faster than traditional methods, but they can result in more fabric waste.

Rotary Cutting Tool Care

- Replace rotary cutter blades often. If the blade can't cut through fabric like a hot knife through butter, replace it.
- Mats used with rotary cutters do wear out over time. If your rotary cutter blade is new and still cuts poorly, replace your mat.
- Help your rotary cutting mats last longer. Use them only on flat surfaces, keep them out of direct sunlight, store mats flat, and never leave them in a vehicle in the hot sun.

Cutting Tips

- Cut one of each item listed in a project, unless otherwise noted.
- When directions say to cut a strip, cut fabric on the cross grain (from selvage to selvage). Cut the strip to the given width and approximately 40" to 44" long.
- Square up and trim your finished units and blocks to size. Use a ruler to verify that the four-patch unit you just made measures exactly the size given; adjust seams or trim the edges as needed. Do the same with finished blocks.
- Use the bias square ruler to square up half-square triangle units; match the diagonal line of the ruler with the seam.

Pressing Tips

- Correct pressing is as important as accurate sewing. If a seam is not fully pressed open, it changes the dimensions of a finished piece.
- Choose iron settings carefully. Heat and steam can distort pieces.
- Remember the differences between ironing (moving the iron back and forth over the fabric to remove wrinkles) and pressing (lifting the iron up and down off the ironing board to avoid shifting pieces or distorting fabric). The techniques yield different results.

Selecting Fabric

Everyone's approach to fabric selection differs. My preference seems to change from project to project, mood to mood. In general, I seek a balance of color and pattern with some continuity and a combination that is pleasing to the eye as a whole, not just as individual pieces of fabric.

Try this approach. Select a focus fabric — one that has at least three colors in it. This piece of fabric should really speak to you and excite you. If you aren't inspired by the main fabric, you aren't going to enjoy making the project; odds are it will then end up in your pile of UFOs (quilter talk for UnFinished Objects).

Use your main fabric as a guide. Choose prints that complement it or bring out your favorite colors. Include a variety of textures, geometrics, florals, stripes, curves, swirls, dots, tone-on-tone prints and marbled and mottled fabrics. Be sure to pick a variety of print sizes, such as large and small floral prints, a medium-sized swirl, a wide stripe and two sizes of geometric prints. Sometimes you'll find only one piece of fabric in just the right color; other times you will have several prints in the right color range, so you can be more particular.

Having some trouble figuring out what color to put with your focus fabric? Look at the selvage of your main print. Most (but not all) fabrics have color dots printed on them, showing the colors used in the production of that fabric. Use those dots as a color guide, like you would use paint samples from your home improvement store.

Audition your fabric choices. Lay them out in front of you, and overlap fabrics so the general proportion of the fabrics is the same as it will be in your project. For example, if one really bright piece of fabric only will be used in 2" squares here and there, show a smaller amount of it during the audition than you would the 12" pieces of sky fabric that will be used behind the animals. Remember that the animals or other fused designs also are part of your overall plan, so test a small piece of each fabric with your collection.

Finally, choose your binding fabric. It can be the same fabric you used in your project, or you can carry another color out to the edge. Binding is a design element that often is overlooked; take advantage of it.

Color Tips

Here are a few things to keep in mind before you head off to select fabrics:

- Use color to set the tone for the piece. Create high contrast between your background fabric and the designs on top of it to help the designs stand out. For instance, pairing navy blue with cream will make designs pop, but matching low-contrast fabrics, such as medium blue and medium green, will create subtle lines and help elements blend together.

- Be creative. Make animals, trees and flowers in any color palette that pleases you rather than restricting yourself to the realistic colors found in nature.

- Let thread make a statement. If a design is fused in place before you decide there isn't enough contrast with the background, add thread work and extra stitching lines to make the contrast. Use a stabilizer if you add the stitching before quilting, or use special threads during the quilting process.

Using Fusible Web

Like quilters' tools, the technology of fusible web is ever-changing and evolving. Your favorite product last year may be unavailable this year, so what do you do? Experiment and improvise!

To make your life easier, here are general instructions and tips on using fusibles, plus some alternatives to fusibles.

Using Fusibles

Note: The designs in this book are reversed for use with fusible web. When complete, the designs in your projects will face the same direction as shown in the photos.

1. Trace appliqué shapes individually onto the paper side of your fusible web, leaving about ½" open area between pieces. Dashed lines on a shape show where pieces will overlap; the dashed area is under another piece.
2. Loosely cut out each piece, about ¼" larger than drawn. Follow the manufacturer's instructions to iron them to the wrong side of your selected fabrics. As a general rule, use a dry iron with most fusibles.
3. Cut out each piece directly on the drawn lines. Remove the paper from each piece.
4. Position the pieces as indicated in the photos or as you like. For complicated designs with many pieces, such as a swan or flower, refer to Using a Nonstick Pressing Sheet. Follow the directions to create a single, moveable appliqué design unit, then continue with the next two steps to position and fuse the unit to your background.
5. Iron pieces in place as directed by the manufacturer.
6. Finish the raw edges of your design. This is an optional step for some fusibles, but it makes the designs more durable and less likely to fray or fall off over time.

Using a Nonstick Pressing Sheet

Note: Create a single design unit with this technique by fusing two or more parts together into one movable appliqué with the help of a nonstick pressing sheet.

1. Follow standard fusible web procedures to cut out each design element, such as all of the leaves and petals of your flower, or the wings, body, beak and feet of a goose.
2. Working on an ironing board, place a nonstick pressing sheet on top of the layout diagram for your design; you should be able to see your layout diagram through your pressing sheet. Place white paper below the layout diagram to improve visibility. Lay your individual pieces out in front of you.
3. Fuse small units together; for example, fuse the two parts of one petal together. Repeat with other petals and with leaves made of two parts. Use tweezers to pick up and place the small pieces. (Not all projects have small units that can be put together like this.)
4. Think of your design as layers. Fuse the lowest layer to the pressing sheet as shown in your layout diagram; build up from there, adding a layer at a time and fusing the layers together often.
5. Repeat this layering process as you add all elements of the design, using your layout diagram as a guide for placement.
6. Let fused appliqué unit cool completely, then peel it off the pressing sheet in one piece. It is now complete and ready to add to your project.

Using a Nonstick Pressing Sheet

Fuse small units together.

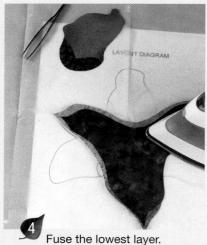
Fuse the lowest layer.

Layer the pieces.

Fusible Web Tips

Before Starting

- Select a fusible web to suit your project. This is the most important choice you will make for any fusible project. I prefer a lightweight product that can be sewn through easily.
- Use only one brand of fusible web in each project. This ensures consistent results.
- Test the product on a scrap of the same fabric you will be using in the finished piece. This is the second most important thing to do to ensure good results. Heat is critical, and a test will help you determine the best iron temperature and pressing time. Each fusible brand is different, and so is each iron; follow the manufacturer's directions, but make adjustments to fit your particular situation. Most call for a dry iron.
- Most fusibles seem to have a shelf life. If you are having problems with your old product, try something newer.
- Store fusible web rolled up in a large roll, rather than tightly wound or folded, to prevent the glued surface from releasing from the paper side during storage. If the layers separate, it is very difficult to use the product as intended.

Cutting

- If you have fused several designs to a large piece of fabric (for example, several trees fused to one fabric), loosely cut them apart, then accurately cut each individual item directly on the drawn lines.

- Use sharp, pointed fabric scissors. Choose small scissors for small items and long-bladed scissors for larger items. Avoid scissors with dull blades; they will tear the fabric and tend to fray it.
- Get clean edges when cutting by holding your scissors stationary and moving the fabric around the scissors as you cut out your design.
- If you cut off a leg or antler or a part of a tree, try to salvage it by overlapping the pieces slightly and fusing them down. Sometimes the area that was cut off can be omitted. Then again, there are times you just have to start over.
- For more lifelike animals, cut areas like the elk's neck with a wiggling motion so the finished look is uneven.
- Simplify cutting detail pieces, such as tiny points on antlers. First, cut up to the base of the antlers and around them in a clump. Then, go back and clip out the area between the tines.
- Take your time. If you have to cut many pieces, break up the monotony and strain by doing a few at a time.
- If you have arthritis, trouble seeing clearly, or poor depth perception, ask a friend to help. Or, offer to trade tasks with a friend, like some of your machine piecing for some of your friend's cutting.

Assembling

- Remove the paper backing from your pieces carefully. The smaller or skinnier the pieces are, the easier it is for the fabric itself to tear as you remove the paper. If the webbing separates as you try to pull off the paper backing, the piece needs to be ironed longer. Re-iron.
- Use tweezers to pick up and place small fusible pieces.
- Lay out all of your design pieces before fusing them in place. Verify alignment by using rulers as needed, allowing for seam allowances.
- For complicated designs or designs made of many pieces, such as the geese or flowers, make a "unit" first before positioning and fusing it to your fabric background. See Using a Nonstick Pressing Sheet for complete directions.
- Handle the cut design pieces as little as possible to minimize fraying.
- Some items can be fused to their background fabric after the piecing is complete. However, if a portion of a design, like a mountain, extends into the seam allowance, fuse it before piecing to ensure the best look.
- Reduce the bulk of fusibles on large designs. Trace your design as usual onto fusible web. Before you fuse it to the selected fabric, trim away excess fusible in the center of the design, leaving ¼" to ½" of fusible on the outer edges only. Now fuse it to the fabric and cut out the design as usual.

Pressing

- Be sure the fusible side of your design faces downward so your iron touches fabric, not fusible web. If needed, clean your iron.
- When working with fusibles, remember to press rather than iron. Moving the iron back and forth, like you would to iron a shirt, will make pieces shift. Pressing, or lifting the iron up off the ironing board, then setting it down in another spot, will allow the iron to accurately set the pieces.
- Fuse designs over seams by pressing seams very flat first, which will prevent puckers as the item is fused into place.
- Shift designs slightly to avoid having the ends or points of designs end on a seam, which can reduce adhesion.
- Clean your iron of melted fusible goo by rubbing the iron (while it is still warm) with a used, nonstatic dryer sheet. Check your local quilt shop for other cleaning products.

Using Pressure-Sensitive Fusible Webs

- Use pressure-sensitive fusible webs, such as Steam-A-Seam 2, in a warm environment.
- If a pressure-sensitive product doesn't stick to the fabric as it should, lightly tack it in place with the tip of an iron; keep the paper side up. Then, cut out the design. Some fabrics may have finishes that don't work with the pressure-sensitive product.
- Once you position pieces using pressure-sensitive fusibles, steam the designs in place, both from the right side of the project and the wrong side. Use a lot of water or steam and a pressing cloth (like cheesecloth).
- Stitch pieces fused with lightweight, pressure-sensitive product to make the fusing permanent. Pieces fused with regular-weight fusible web are fine without stitching.

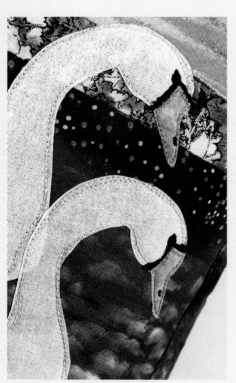

Finishing Your Fusibles

Are you worried about raw edges? Lifting seams? Pieces coming loose? There are several basic ways to finish the raw edges of your fused designs. Here are some ideas and examples. If you don't find the finish you want, check Alternatives to Fusibles.

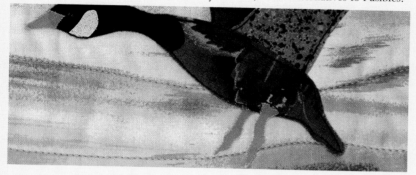

Unfinished Raw Edges

Unfinished raw edges are best for items that won't be washed or handled a lot. Choose a fusible known for its durability and strong adhesion, like Steam-A-Seam 2.

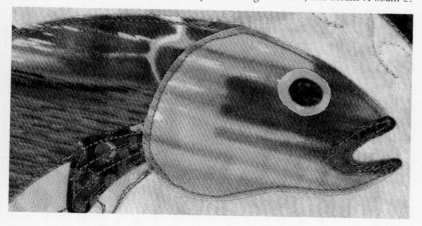

Straight-Stitched Raw Edges (Machine)

Straight stitch raw edges by free motion. Drop the feed dogs, use a darning foot and stitch a scant ⅛" inside each design. For simpler designs, sew with a regular stitch (feed dogs up), and use a standard foot or walking foot. This can be sewn through the design and background using a tear-away stabilizer, or sewn during the machine quilting process through all layers. This method, which is the one I use most often, works best when raw edges are meant to show, yet the design pieces need to be attached permanently. Raw edges may fray somewhat when washed. The stitching line can become an added visual element in the finished project. This is the method I use most often.

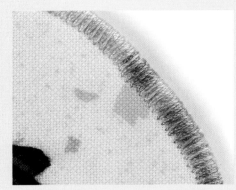

Zigzag or Satin-Stitched Raw Edges (Machine)

Use a standard zigzag stitch that is shortened in length and narrowed in width, generally with a stabilizer. Test your settings to find what you like. Keep the stitch in proportion to the size of the pieces being sewn down. Use a tear-away stabilizer and stitch through the design, background and stabilizer before quilting.

This method works best to securely anchor design pieces in place. It takes longer to stitch, but compared with other finishes, it holds up the best to repeated washing. This also is the method used to finish the raw edges of coasters, and it generally is done without stabilizer.

Blanket Stitched Raw Edges (Machine or Hand)

Many newer sewing machines include a blanket stitch (check your manual), but this also is a fun embroidery stitch to sew by hand. When sewing this stitch by machine, use two threads or a single, heavier thread to get a professional look.

When sewing the blanket stitch by hand, use 16" to 18" lengths of two or three strands of embroidery floss. Take the majority of the stitch on the background fabric, a needle's width away from the design. Then take a single stitch on the design. Repeat. Make stitches at a 90-degree angle to the design's outer edge and in proportion to the design piece. Take shorter and/or smaller stitches around antlers or skinny legs.

This method is used to secure designs in place and add a folk-art charm to your piece. Raw edges still may fray some with washing, but the stitching holds designs in place permanently.

Raw Edges Covered With Sheer Fabric and Stitched (Machine or Hand)

This technique wasn't used with any of the projects in this book, but it is an option for wall hangings and pillows. Don't use this method with an item that will be washed and handled a lot.

After design elements are fused in place, lay a piece of organza, sheer fabric or netting over the top of the whole block. Sew through the sheer fabric and around — but not directly on — each fused design. By machine, sew with free-motion machine stitching and use a stabilizer. By hand, sew a running stitch and hide knots on the back of your fabric. This stitch also can be sewn during the machine quilting process through all layers.

Use this method to securely anchor design pieces in place. Pieces generally will wash well, if shrinkage has been considered for all fabrics. The color of the sheer fabric will affect the depth of color in the fused designs, but it can be an interesting element in the overall design. Experiment!

Alternatives to Fusibles

Many of the finishing methods described in the previous section can be adapted to no-fuse alternatives, but they may require additional steps, such as reversing a design. Here are some no-fuse options and techniques. Also, consider using temporary spray adhesive, an alternative to both fusibles and pins.

Reversing a Design

Sometimes, a design needs to be reversed. If your design is symmetrical, or if you don't care if a design faces right or left, you can skip this tip. Otherwise, trace your chosen design on one side of a piece of paper, then place it on a light table or window to copy the design onto the back of your paper. This new, reversed design is the one that you will use as your pattern.

Traditional Appliqué (Hand)

Make a template for each design out of template plastic or freezer paper. Trace the design onto the wrong side of your fabric, cutting it out a scant ¼" larger than drawn. Position the piece on the project, turn the raw edges under, and sew it with your favorite appliqué method.

Freezer Paper Template: Reversed Design (Machine or Hand)

Option 1: Start by reversing designs. Refer to Reversing a Design for details. Trace the designs onto the paper side of freezer paper, then cut them out. Iron the freezer paper to the right side of the fabric. Cut out fused pieces a scant ¼" larger than the template. Remove the freezer paper. Position the design on the project. Turn the raw edges under, and appliqué by hand or machine, using your favorite stitch.

Option 2: Follow the same steps as Option 1, except add these steps before positioning and appliquéing the piece. Peel the freezer paper off of the right side of the fabric. Place the freezer paper shiny side up on the wrong side of the fabric, centering the freezer paper template on the design. Iron the seam allowance to the freezer paper around all edges, creating a clean, finished edge. Iron the piece in place on the background; appliqué by hand or machine. Cut a slit in the backing material below the design. Remove the freezer paper.

Option 3: Rather than pinning pieces in place, spray the pieces with a temporary adhesive spray, then position them on the project. Appliqué to finish.

Tracing With a Permanent Marker

When a project calls for extremely tiny pieces, such as nostrils, eyes and talons, it makes sense to draw or stitch these details rather than fuse them in place. If you choose drawing, trace the design directly onto fabric using the diagram provided with your pattern. You may need to use a light box or place the pattern and fabric in a window. Use a permanent marking pen, such as those used in scrapbooking. I prefer Pigma Micron pens in sizes 05 or 03.

When possible, I trace these details onto my fabric pieces before they are fused in place, in case I'm not happy with the work and want to redo it. For the goose nostril, swan eye or swan nostril, these details can be added after the bird unit has been fused together and before it is attached to the background. The talon of the eagle is part of a larger fused piece; color in the talon portion before it is fused in place as you would if you used crayons.

Follow the marking pen manufacturer's directions. Often, you will need to press the area with a dry iron to make the ink permanent.

Piecing Techniques

Here are detailed instructions on speed-piecing techniques used in the projects of this book.

Half-Square Triangles

Every pair of squares will yield a pair of identical half-square triangles.

1. Cut an equal number of light and dark squares of the same size. Use this formula: Finished Size of Square + ⅞" = Size of Squares to Start With. I prefer to cut my squares 1" larger than finished size, which gives me a little margin for error. Any excess is trimmed away later.
2. Mark a diagonal line on the wrong side of each light fabric.
3. Place one light and one dark square right sides together.
4. Stitch ¼" away from the drawn line, on both sides of the line.
5. Cut on the drawn line.
6. Press seams to the dark side.
7. Square up pieces to the correct size, trimming off points. I use the bias square ruler for this step, aligning the 45-degree angle on the seam line.

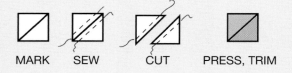

MARK   SEW   CUT   PRESS, TRIM

Speedy Triangles

This is a fun and easy way to add a triangle to a rectangle or square without actually working with a triangle. It has several other names, such as fast-corner triangles, quick triangles, connector squares, etc. It is quick and simple and pretty accurate, but it does have some waste.

1. Place the fabric for the triangle (currently a square) right sides together in the corner of the square or rectangle to which it is added.
2. On the wrong side of the triangle fabric, draw a diagonal line from corner to corner.
3. Sew on the diagonal line.
4. Trim off the outside corner of the triangle fabric only. Don't trim the original square or rectangle.
5. Press to the corner.

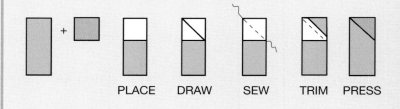

PLACE   DRAW   SEW   TRIM   PRESS

Four-Patch Blocks

Each block is a simple checkerboard, made from two strips: one light and one dark. Two segments are sewn together to form each four-patch. Refer to Checkerboards for directions.

Checkerboards

Checkerboards for projects in this book are pieced with a speed technique using strips of fabric rather than many small squares. The actual strip sizes will be given in each project. There is room for some error in cutting, but not a lot.

1. Sew alternating strips of light and dark fabrics together along their length; use an accurate ¼" seam.
2. Press toward the dark fabric.
3. For accuracy, verify that this pressed unit is the correct width as listed in your project; adjust the stitching if necessary.
4. Cut across these strips to make smaller segments. The actual size to cross-cut will be given in your project, but it is usually the same measurement as the width of the initial strips.
5. Sew the segments together, alternating color placement and forming a checkerboard. A completed checkerboard strip is a single row of squares of a specified length, such as one square by eight squares.
6. Press the seams in one direction, or press them open.

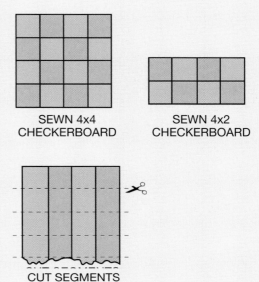

SEWN 4x4 CHECKERBOARD SEWN 4x2 CHECKERBOARD

CUT SEGMENTS

Fast Flying Geese

Sew together one large square and four small squares in this speed method to yield four flying geese units of identical color and size.

1. Cut the squares needed for your project. There will be a ratio of four small squares to one large square. Draw a diagonal line on the wrong side of every small square; use whatever tool works best for that fabric (sharp No. 2 pencil, white chalk pencil or colored pencil).
2. Lay one large square right side up in front of you. Place one small square right sides together in one corner and diagonally opposite, aligning edges and drawn lines. Their points will overlap in the middle.
3. Sew ¼" away from the drawn line, on both sides of the line. Cut on the drawn line.
4. Press toward the smaller pieces.
5. Lay a small square right sides together in the remaining 90-degree corner of the large triangle. The point and drawn line of the small square should extend between the two sewn triangles.
6. Sew ¼" away from the drawn line, on both sides of it. Cut on the drawn line. Press toward the smaller piece. Repeat. Trim points.
7. Trim to the correct size as listed in your project directions.

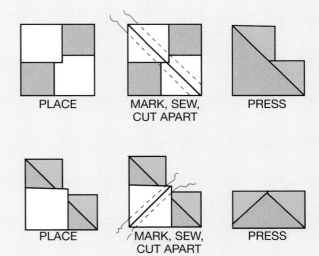

PLACE MARK, SEW, CUT APART PRESS

PLACE MARK, SEW, CUT APART PRESS

Customizing Projects

Let your creativity come out to play, and make the projects in this book your own. But how do you get from that idea phase to the "Aah! Look what I've done!" phase?

Start by jotting down the elements you like the most and your requirements, like a "wants and needs" list. Maybe you need a gift for a graduating relative, and he likes deer. How big do you want the quilt or wall hanging to be? How much time do you have to complete it? How much of your time do you want to invest in its construction? How much money do you want to spend? What kind of finishing technique will you do? What's your skill level or area of expertise? Make notes of all of these things to start.

Here are some other quick tips for customizing projects:

Altering the Look

Embellishing is a great way to customize your project. Check the projects featured in this book; you'll see decorative stitching added to birds, animals, leaves and trees. There also are some choices that add dimension, such as buttons and real fishing tackle. Without these finishing details, the designs are very simple. Experiment with the stitch options on your sewing machine and the wonderful thread choices that are available. Many of the same details can be added by hand embroidery, if that's your specialty. Either way, with the right tools and equipment, these intricate details nearly happen on their own. Experiment with stitches on a small project first, like a coaster, napkin or place mat. Once you're happy with the thread and stitching, apply this treatment to your larger project.

Changing an Edge Finish

To make a project as shown but change how the raw edges of fused designs are finished, refer to the tips in the Fusible Web section. You'll find a lot of helpful tips and options, plus alternatives to fusibles.

Changing Elements in a Project

Many project elements are interchangeable. For example, it's easy to substitute one 12" x 14" scene for another. Many animals also can be moved around, but look for good proportion with your new choices. If you plan to make coordinating items, be sure to purchase extra yardage so everything matches.

Making a Project Larger

Want to modify a wall hanging to fit a bed? Let some basic questions guide your decisions. How big is the wall hanging compared with your needed quilt size? Would you like to use the wall hanging as a medallion in the center of the bed quilt, surrounded by borders or piecing? Do you want to enlarge the overall size of the wall hanging to be more in proportion to the finished quilt, or can you make more blocks to enlarge the overall design? Will you make pillows to match the quilt, or a table runner and coordinating place mats? These are all considerations, and the yardages required for each will depend on your choices. Use the information and sizes I have provided as a starting point; then sharpen your pencil and get the calculator out. When in doubt, purchase extra yardage. (You don't really need an excuse, do you?)

Adding Borders

The projects in this book all have borders that are appropriate for each, according to my taste. However, I encourage you to make changes to your project as you see fit. Every fabric is different, and every quilter is unique; what I think looks just right may need adjustment in your opinion. Feel free to make these changes.

Choosing Fabric

Audition your border fabric before you commit to using it. Position your chunk of fabric behind the completed top, or cut strips and arrange them according to the diagrams provided. Does the chosen print add to the overall design? Does it overpower the rest of the project? Would a narrower border be better? How about adding a narrow inner border? Choices, choices, choices. When you modify a design, the pattern becomes a suggestion, not a directive.

Measuring

1. Square up your quilt top before adding borders. The goal of squaring up your piece is for the top's outer edges to be straight and to make a clean, 90-degree angle at all four corners. Any inner seam lines need to be straight in relation to the edge. Place a large, square ruler (such as a 15" square) in one corner of the top. Look at where the lines on the ruler align with seams on the top, and compare the edge of your top and the straight edge of the ruler. Do the lines and edges match up? If so, fantastic! If not, make adjustments to the seams or pressing.

2. Measure through the center of your project from top to bottom; this tells you the length of side borders. Compare that length to the actual measurement of each side; if the numbers are widely different, look at your seams and make adjustments to your top before adding borders. When the length measured through the center and measured at the sides is the same or very close, you are ready to cut your side borders. Don't be tempted to cut a length of border fabric, sew it onto the side of your top and whack it off where it meets the other end of your top. This almost certainly will guarantee wavy edges in the end.

3. After you add the side borders, repeat this process for the top and bottom borders, measuring from side to side. Compare this measurement to actual edge measurements, and make adjustments as needed.

Cutting

1. Cut your border pieces. If you are cutting along the cross grain (from selvage to selvage), cut to the length of the center measurement, but exclude selvages from this length. Borders cut this way may stretch a little, but this is the most economical use of your fabric; pin pieces well to avoid problems. Material requirements are given for borders cut on the cross grain. For more stability, cut borders along the straight of grain (parallel to the selvage) to the length of the center measurement. You will need to buy more fabric than listed. The larger the quilt top, the more important it is to have a stable outer border so the quilt hangs properly.

2. To connect border strips to reach the desired border length, place two strips right sides together, and sew a ¼" seam on the narrow side of the strip. While binding strips are sewn together at a 45-degree angle, borders usually are not. Press the seams open, and cut the border length needed. Exclude selvages from your border strips.

Sewing

1. Square up your quilt top as described in Measuring.

2. Sew a border to each side of your top. Press seams toward the border. Square up each corner the same way you squared up the top before the borders.

3. Sew a border to the top and bottom of the quilt top. Press seams toward the border. Square up each corner.

4. Be consistent in how you add the pieces. If you stitched the sides of your inner border first, then add the sides of your outer border

Quilting the Top

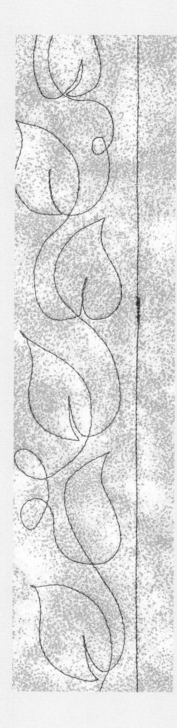

1. Press your completed project and quilt back. Use steam if it is needed; a flat top is more accurately and easily quilted.

2. If you haven't already done so, square up your quilt top. (See Adding Borders.)

3. Decide how you will quilt your project. Use your favorite method to mark quilting lines, if needed, but test your marking methods for visibility and ease in removal. Look at photos of each project for ideas, or see Quilting Designs.

4. Select batting. For wall hangings, table runners and place mats, I prefer Warm & Natural by The Warm Company. This 100 percent cotton batting hangs well, gives the project a nice feel and machine quilts easily. For lap quilts, I prefer Soft & Bright, also by The Warm Company. This needled polyester batting washes well, has a nice loft and is easy to work with.

5. Cut the backing and batting about 4" larger than the size of a wall hanging project, or even larger for bigger projects (or as required by your machine quilter). For example, if my top measures 40" x 40", I would cut the backing and batting to measure 44" x 44".

6. Lay the backing on a flat surface, wrong side up. Use your kitchen table, a tile floor or two conference tables pushed together. If you need more space, ask to use your local quilt shop's classroom space and tables.

7. Tape or clamp the edges down at approximately 4" intervals, keeping the backing flat and taut but not over-stretched. Remove any lint or threads.

8. Center and smooth the batting over the backing, or use a temporary spray adhesive to hold the layers together. Do not pin or tape the batting. Remove any lint or foreign objects from the batting surface.

9. Center and smooth the pressed quilt top, right side up, over the batting. Or, use a temporary spray adhesive to hold the layers together.

10. If you are using a temporary spray adhesive, skip to the next step. Otherwise, baste the pieces together with pins, a basting tool or thread. Begin in the center and work outward, basting every 2" to 3", depending on the batting used. Most batting packages specify the minimum quilting required. If in doubt, ask your local quilt shop.

11. Remove the tape, clamps and clips.

12. Quilt the sandwiched top, batting and backing by hand or machine. Begin in the center and work outward. The amount of quilting should be consistent throughout, rather than being dense in one area and hardly stitched in another.

13. Remove any remaining basting pins, thread or marked guidelines.

14. Square up the quilted project, trimming the backing and batting to size. Your quilt is now ready to bind.

Quilting Designs

Quilting is an integral design element in your project. It can add to the impact of your pattern and fabric choices, or it can accentuate a problem. It can become a major contributing detail in the overall project, or it can become the focal point. It can blend, soften and soothe, or it can distort, distract and agitate.

So how do you select the right quilting for each project? Ask yourself these questions:
- What is the purpose of the quilt or project?
- Who is it for?
- How will it be used or displayed?
- Will it be washed and handled a lot?
- How much quilting is required for the batting used?
- Do I have blank areas to fill in with quilting?
- Do I have the skill level to do what I want?

Ultimately, the amount and type of quilting you add is your personal decision. Look at the quilting I've done for the projects in this book and in the designs below. You also can use the animals, birds, fish, flowers and trees in this book as quilting templates.

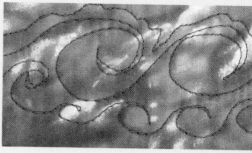

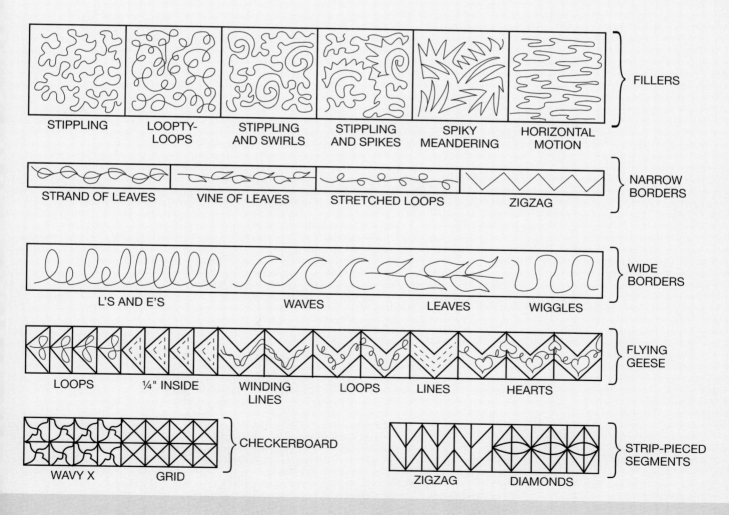

FILLERS: STIPPLING, LOOPTY-LOOPS, STIPPLING AND SWIRLS, STIPPLING AND SPIKES, SPIKY MEANDERING, HORIZONTAL MOTION

NARROW BORDERS: STRAND OF LEAVES, VINE OF LEAVES, STRETCHED LOOPS, ZIGZAG

WIDE BORDERS: L'S AND E'S, WAVES, LEAVES, WIGGLES

FLYING GEESE: LOOPS, ¼" INSIDE, WINDING LINES, LOOPS, LINES, HEARTS

CHECKERBOARD: WAVY X, GRID

STRIP-PIECED SEGMENTS: ZIGZAG, DIAMONDS

Binding and Finishing

My favorite binding method is a double-fold technique, which begins with 2¼" strips cut on the cross grain. Many quilters use 2½" strips, so yardage amounts for binding projects in this book are based on this width. Strips are sewn together with a 45-degree angle and pressed open to reduce bulk. I often overlap the ends of the binding, but other methods work equally well.

1. Cut enough strips on the cross grain (selvage to selvage) to go around your project plus about 8". Bind curved edges with a bias binding. Cut strips on the bias instead of on the cross grain.

2. Sew the strips right sides together at a 45-degree angle. Trim the seams to ¼". Press open.

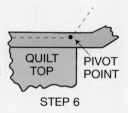

STEP 2

3. Press the long binding strip in half, wrong sides together, making it approximately 1¼" wide.

4. Cut one end at a 45-degree angle. Press under ¼" to finish the edge. This is your beginning edge.

STEP 4

5. Place the beginning edge of your binding on the quilt top at the center bottom (or at an inconspicuous spot); keep raw edges even. Begin sewing through all layers approximately 3" from this point, using a ¼" seam and backstitching.

6. Sew to ¼" from the first corner. Pivot with the needle down at this point, and continue sewing out at a 45-degree angle to the corner of the quilt. Clip the threads. Remove the quilt from the machine — don't backstitch.

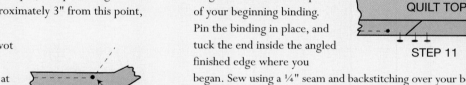

QUILT TOP   PIVOT POINT

STEP 6

7. Fold the binding away from you, as shown in the diagram. The 45-degree angle sewn will help you fold this correctly.

QUILT TOP   45° ANGLE

STEP 7

8. Fold the binding down toward you; align the top edge of the folded binding with the top edge of your quilt. The raw edges of the binding and right side of the quilt top should align.

QUILT TOP

STEP 8

9. Beginning at the outer edge, sew a ¼" seam. Continue to the next corner.

10. Repeat Steps 6 through 9 until you complete all four corners.

11. Trim excess binding to ½" longer than the farthest point of your beginning binding. Pin the binding in place, and tuck the end inside the angled finished edge where you began. Sew using a ¼" seam and backstitching over your beginning stitches.

QUILT TOP

STEP 11

12. For wall hangings, add a hanging sleeve. Fold the binding to the back of the quilt. Use a blind stitch to sew the binding in place by hand.

Labels

Add a label to your quilt to identify the maker, date, pattern and purpose. Labels can be simple or elaborate, pieced into the quilt back or hand-sewn to the back after quilting. Whatever you choose, labels add a great finishing touch to a project and are a wonderful memento.

Hanging Sleeves

Add a sleeve to your wall hanging after the binding is machine sewn to the quilt, but before it is hand stitched down.

1. Cut a 6" strip of fabric that coordinates with the quilt back and measures 1½" narrower than the quilt.

2. Turn the narrow edges under ¼". Press.

3. Fold the strip in half along the length, wrong sides together. Press. Your sleeve is now 3" wide.

4. Center the sleeve on quilt back, aligning the sleeve's raw edges with the top's raw edges.

5. Sew through all layers on the same stitching line as the binding. Backstitch at the beginning and end. This seam is covered when the binding is hand-stitched in place.

6. Use a blind stitch to sew the folded edge in place by hand. The hand stitching should not show on the front of the quilt.

Chapter 2
Fur

Grouped in this chapter are projects featuring deer, moose and bear. Sew a table runner and a matching set of place mats, napkins and coasters. Make a coordinating throw and pillow. Even simpler, add the animal designs to purchased towels. Whatever your choice, carry your theme throughout your home with these projects. Review the Glossary for explanations on terminology; see Chapter 1 for general tips on basting, quilting, binding and using fusibles.

  Fur

Cut

Fabric	Size	How Many	For
A	6½" squares	5	Background
B	3½" squares	4	Background
C	2½" x 24½"	2	Inner border
D	2½" x 28½"	2	Inner border
E	4½" x 28½"	2	Outer border
F	4½" x 36½"	2	Outer border
Medium checkerboard	3½"-wide strips	2	Checkerboard squares
	2½" squares	4	Speedy triangles
Dark checkerboard	3½"-wide strips	2	Checkerboard squares
	2½" squares	4	Speedy triangles
Binding	2½"-wide strips	4	Binding

Finished size: 36" x 36".

You Will Need

- ⅝ yd. print fabric (outer border)
- 1 yd. dark fabric (inner border, checkerboards, binding)
- ¼ yd. medium fabric (checkerboards)
- ⅓ yd. light fabric (background)
- ¼ yd. dark fabric (deer heads, hoof prints)
- 1½ yd. fabric (quilt back, hanging sleeve)
- 1¼ yd. batting
- ½ yd. fusible web
- Thread
- Appliqué patterns: Fur 1, Fur 2, Fur 3.
- General sewing tools (Chapter 1)

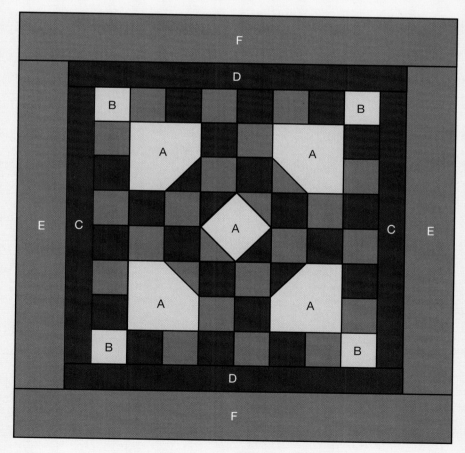

Racks and Tracks Wall Hanging Layout Diagram

Construction and Quilting

1. Refer to the Layout Diagram to position each piece of your wall hanging on a design wall or other work surface. Refer to the Construction Diagram as you prepare to sew. For more detailed instructions or specific techniques used in this project, refer to Chapter 1.

2. Sew four-patch blocks and checkerboards following the directions in Chapter 1. Use 3½"-wide strips cut from medium and dark checkerboard fabrics.

3. Cut 20 segments, each 3½" wide, from the sewn pairs of strips.

4. From the segments, create four different four-patch blocks. Each block should measure 6½" square. Place the finished blocks on the design wall.

5. From the segments, make four checkerboard strips that are one block tall x six squares long. Place two checkerboard strips on the design wall.

6. Add one B square to the ends of two checkerboard strips. Call each Unit B. Position these on the design wall.

7. Sew speedy triangles. Use A squares and 2½" squares cut from the checkerboard fabrics.

8. Before removing pieces from your design wall, pin a note to each A piece to mark each corner where a medium or dark square should be sewn. To use directional prints for 2½" squares, pin folded squares to A before sewing. View the pieces in place on a design wall to verify the directional print is correct.

9. Sew one square to each of four A pieces. Sew four squares to one A piece. Refer to the Layout Diagram. Press the seams toward the added piece; trim if desired.

10. Return the completed pieces to the design wall.

11. Refer to the Construction Diagram, and sew blocks in Row 1 together. Press the seams toward the four-patch block. Repeat for Rows 2 and 3.

12. Sew Row 1 + Row 2 + Row 3. Press the seams open or in one direction.

13. Add a checkerboard strip to each side. Add Unit B to the top and bottom. Press the seams away from the center.

14. Square up the piece to 24½" x 24½".

15. Add borders in alphabetical order, pressing each seam toward the border. Square up the piece after adding D and square up again after adding F.

16. Trace and cut out the appliqué deer heads and hoof prints; follow the fusible web manufacturer's directions. Cut two Fur 1 appliqués, three Fur 2 appliqués and four Fur 3 appliqués.

17. Fuse the designs in place. Finish the raw edges as you prefer.

18. Quilt, embellish and bind the quilt as desired.

19. Add a hanging sleeve and label.

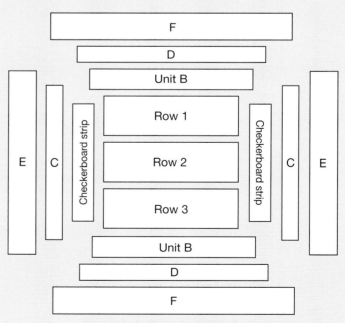

Racks and Tracks Wall Hanging
Construction Diagram

   Fur

Variation: Racks and Tracks Wall Hanging

Cut

Fabric	Size	How Many	For
A	6½" squares	4	Background
B	3½" squares	4	Background
C	2½" x 24½"	2	Inner border
D	2½" x 28½"	2	Inner border
E	3½" x 28½"	2	Outer border
F	3½" x 34½"	2	Outer border
Medium checkerboard	3½"-wide strips	2	Checkerboard squares
	2½" squares	4	Speedy triangles
Dark checkerboard	3½"-wide strips	2	Checkerboard squares
	2½" squares	4	Speedy triangles
Binding fabric	2½"-wide strips	4	Binding

Finished size: 34" x 34".

You Will Need

- ⅔ yd. dark fabric (outer border, checkerboards)
- 1 yd. medium fabric (inner border, checkerboards, binding)
- ⅓ yd. light fabric (background)
- ¼ yd. dark fabric (deer heads, hoof prints)
- 1½ yd. fabric (quilt back, hanging sleeve)
- 1¼ yd. batting
- ½ yd. fusible web
- Thread
- Appliqué patterns:
  Fur 1, Fur 3, Fur 4, Fur 5, Fur 6
- General sewing tools (Chapter 1)

Construction and Quilting

Follow the steps for the Racks and Tracks Wall Hanging, changing these steps:

1. Refer to the Variation: Racks and Tracks Wall Hanging Layout Diagram. The Construction Diagram is the same for both projects.

3. Cut 22 segments, each 3½".

4. Make five four-patch blocks.

9. For speedy triangles, add one medium square and one dark square to adjacent corners of each A piece. Sew two with the medium print on left and two with the medium print on right. Refer to the Layout Diagram.

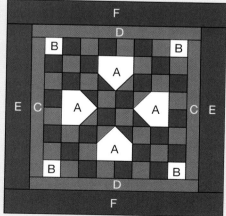

Variation: Racks and Tracks Wall Hanging Layout Diagram

Cut

Fabric	Size	How Many	For
A	6½" square	4	Background
Medium checkerboard	3½"-wide strips	1	Checkerboard squares
	2½" squares	4	Speedy triangles
Dark checkerboard	3½"-wide strips	1	Checkerboard squares
	2½" squares	4	Speedy triangles
Piping fabric	2"-wide strips	2	Piping
Fabric of choice	19" square	1	Pillow back

Finished size: 18" square. Fabrics by P&B Textiles.

Construction

Follow the construction steps for Racks and Tracks Wall Hanging, with changes to these steps:

1. Refer to the Northern Exposure Pillows Layout Diagram.
3. Cut 10 segments, each 3½".
4. Make five four-patch blocks.
5. Speedy triangles: Add one medium square and one dark square to adjacent corners of each A piece. Sew two with the medium print on the left and two with the medium print on the right. Refer to the Layout Diagram.

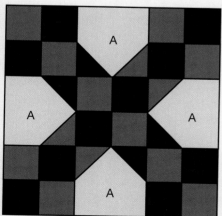

Northern Exposure Pillows
Layout Diagram

Continue pillow construction as follows:

1. Square up the piece to 18½" square.
2. Trace, cut out and fuse the moose head or deer head appliqués. Finish the raw edges as you prefer.
3. If desired, make piping. Skip this step if you are using purchased piping. Remove selvages from piping fabric strips. Sew the lengths together with a 45-degree seam (like binding strips); press the seam open. Place this length of fabric wrong side up; lay the cording in the center. Fold fabric over the cording, raw edges even, to enclose the cording. Sew close to the cording using a zipper foot.
4. Baste the piping to the right side of the pillow top. Align the raw edges, and sew a gentle curve at the corners. Clip the seam allowance of the piping as needed. Trim away excess cording where ends overlap.
5. Use a ⅜" seam to sew the pillow top right sides together to the pillow back. Leave a 12"- to 13"-wide opening in the bottom. Turn the piece right side out. Press.
6. Insert the pillow form.
7. Whipstitch the opening closed.

You Will Need

(For One Pillow)
- ¼ yd. light fabric (background)
- ¼ yd. medium fabric (checkerboards)
- ¼ yd. dark fabric (checkerboards)
- ¼ yd. dark fabric (moose or deer head appliqués)
- ⅝ yd. fabric of choice (pillow back)
- 18" pillow form
- ¼ yd. fusible web
- 3 yd. purchased piping, or ⅛ yd. fabric and 2¼ yd. of ⅛"- to ¼"-wide cording
- Thread
- Appliqué patterns: Fur 7 and Fur 8
- General sewing tools (Chapter 1)

Tip

The fabric strips used to cover the cording may seem excessively wide, but they are easier to work with. If desired, trim away the excess fabric after the pillow top and back are sewn together and before the piece is turned right side out. Clip the seam allowance of piping at the corners as it is basted in place. Stitch the pillow top and back together, sewing on top of the basting stitch or taking a wider seam so basting stitches do not show. Piping adds a wonderful touch to pillows, but it takes time and patience to sew it in place professionally.

Northern Exposure Throw

  Fur

Cut

Fabric	Size	How Many	For
A	6½" squares	6	Background
B	6½" squares	12	Large squares
C	1½" x 42½"	2	Inner border
D	1½" x 32½"	2	Inner border
E**	3½" x 44½"	2	Outer border
F**	3½" x 38½"	2	Outer border
Medium checkerboard	3½"-wide strips	3	Checkerboard
Dark checkerboard	3½"-wide strips	3	Checkerboard
Binding**	2½"-wide strips	5	Binding

**Note: Cut on the straight of grain, parallel to selvage.

Finished size: 38" x 50".
Fabrics by P&B Textiles; machine quilted by Dawn Kelly.

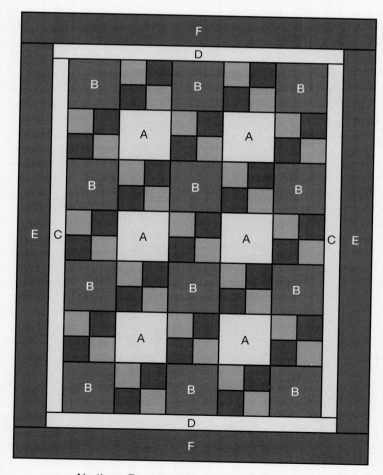

Northern Exposure Throw Layout Diagram

You Will Need

- 1½ yd. dark fabric* (outer border, binding)
- ¼ yd. light fabric (inner border)
- ½ yd. dark floral fabric (large squares)
- ½ yd. light fabric (background)
- ⅓ yd. dark fabric (checkerboards)
- ⅓ yd. medium fabric (checkerboards)
- ¼ yd. dark fabric (moose heads)
- 1½ yd. fabric (quilt back)
- 1¼ yd. batting, 54" wide or greater
- ½ yd. fusible web
- Thread
- Appliqué pattern: Fur 8
- General sewing tools (Chapter 1)

*Note: The yardage amount is enough to cut border and binding pieces on the straight of grain (along the length of the fabric and parallel to the selvage). Cut border pieces first; then cut binding strips from the remaining yardage. Optional: purchase 1 yd. of fabric, cut borders and binding on the cross grain, and piece the borders.

Construction and Quilting

1. Refer to the Layout Diagram. Place A, B and border pieces on a design wall or other work surface. Refer to the Construction Diagram as you prepare to sew.

2. Trace and cut out moose heads, following the fusible web manufacturer's directions. Fuse appliqués in place on A pieces. Finish the raw edges as desired. Return the A pieces to the design wall.

3. Sew the four-patch blocks following the checkerboard instructions in Chapter 1. Use the 3½" strips cut from medium and dark checkerboard fabrics.

4. Cut 34 segments, each 3½", from the sewn pairs of strips.

5. Make 17 four-patch blocks using these segments. Each block should measure 6½" square. Place the blocks on the design wall.

6. Sew each row of five blocks together as shown in the Construction Diagram. Press the seams open.

7. Sew the rows together, pressing seams open or in one direction. Square up the piece; see Chapter 1 for details.

8. Add the borders in alphabetical order, pressing each seam away from the center. Square up the piece after adding D. Square up the piece again after adding F.

9. Quilt, embellish and bind the throw as desired.

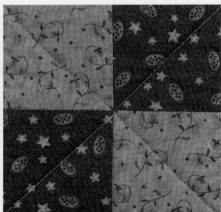

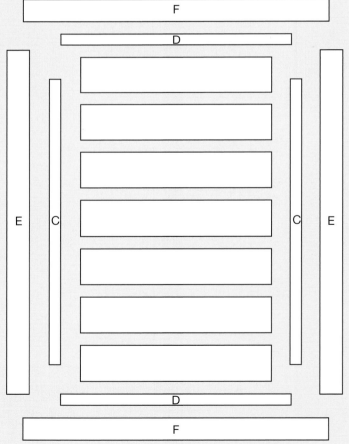

Northern Exposure Throw Construction Diagram

Fur

Northern Exposure Throw

Cut

From	Size	How Many	For
Background fabric	6¼" circle	1	Background
Cotton batting	7" square	1	Batting
Insulated batting	7" square	1	Insulating layer
Backing fabric	7" square	1	Backing
Binding fabric*	2½"-wide strip	1	Bias binding

Note: The potholder can be adapted to a square shape, if you prefer. See the Wild Wings Potholder for general directions for a square potholder.

* Cut the binding strip on the bias, which is at a 45-degree angle from the selvage edge.

Finished size: 6¼" in diameter.

Construction and Quilting

1. Fuse your chosen design to the right side of the background fabric to create the potholder top. Finish the raw edges as desired.

2. Place the potholder top right side up on traditional cotton batting. Quilt as desired. Trim the batting to align with the potholder top. This is now the quilted top.

3. Make a quilt sandwich: Quilted top, right side up + insulated batting + potholder

back, wrong side up. Quilt as desired.

4. Sew around the outer edges of the circle through all layers, using a ⅜" seam allowance. Trim the sandwich to align with the potholder top.

5. Bind the potholder as you would a quilt, except start the binding where the hanging loop will be. For the round potholder, make a bias binding (see Chapter 1) or use purchased bias tape. Sew the binding by machine as normal, except extend the tail of binding 3" beyond the overlap. Turn the binding over the raw edges, and sew it down by hand.

6. Fold the binding tail so no raw edges show; topstitch along the length. Make a loop with the binding, and sew it down with a zigzag stitch.

Tip

If you're not sure where to put the loop, hold your potholder in the air at the point where you think the loop should go. If the design hangs crooked, try again!

You Will Need

(For One Potholder)

- 7" x 7" light scrap (background)
- 7" x 7" brown scrap (appliqué)
- 7" x 7" print (backing)
- Medium-print fat quarter (bias binding strips) or purchased bias tape at least ½" wide
- 7" x 7" specialty insulated batting
- 7" x 7" cotton batting
- 7" x 7" fusible web
- Decorative thread
- Appliqué patterns: Fur 1 and Fur 8
- General sewing tools (Chapter 1)

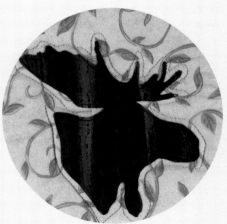

Moose Mountain Wall Hanging

  Fur

Cut

Fabric	Size	How Many	For
A	14½" x 12½"	1	Background
B	6½" x 12½"	1	Inner border
C*	2½" x 20½"	1	Inner border
D*	2½" x 4½"	1	Filler piece
E*	2½" x 18½"	2	Outer border
F*	2½" x 28½"	2	Outer border
Light checkerboard	2½"-wide strips	2	Checkerboard
Medium checkerboard	2½"-wide strips	2	Checkerboard
Binding fabric	2½"-wide strips	3	Binding

*Note: Cut four strips of dark border fabric, each 2½" wide. From these strips, cut C, D, E and F.

Finished size: 28" x 22".

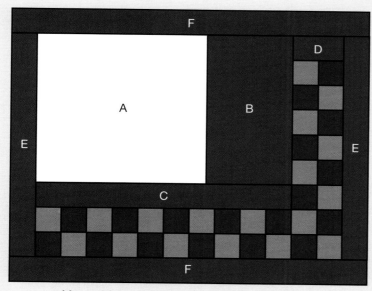

Moose Mountain Wall Hanging Layout Diagram

You Will Need

- 1 light fat quarter (background)
- 1 yd. dark fabric (borders, binding)
- ¼ yd. light fabric (checkerboards)
- ¼ yd. medium fabric (checkerboards)
- 1 dark fat quarter (moose)
- ¼ yd. medium fabric (large grassy area in foreground)
- 4 pieces, each 10" x 10" (one tree, three mountains)
- Fabric scraps (small moose, geese, tree branches, shadowed leg of large moose)
- 1 yd. fabric (quilt back, hanging sleeve)
- ¾ yd. batting
- 1 yd. fusible web
- Thread
- Appliqué patterns: Fur 12, Fur 13, Fur 13a, Fur 14, Fur 17, Fur 18, Fur 38, Fur 39, Fur 40, Fur 41, Fur 42
- General sewing tools (Chapter 1)

Note: Unless otherwise indicated, fabrics need a usable width of 40" or more. The mountains have simple curves and easily can be hand appliquéd if you prefer; refer to Chapter 1. Align grainline markings on mountain pieces with directional prints; this will make the mountains more realistic.

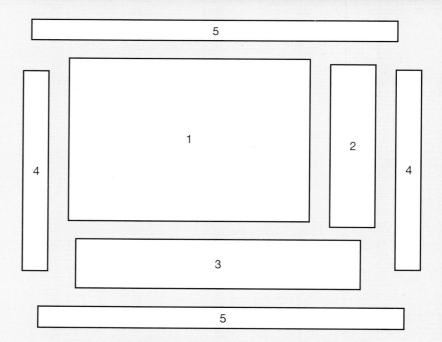

Moose Mountain Wall Hanging Construction Diagram

Fur

Construction and Quilting

1. Refer to the Layout Diagram to position each piece of your wall hanging on a design wall or other work surface. Refer to the Construction Diagram as you prepare to sew. See Chapter 1 for details.

2. Trace and cut out appliqué designs following the fusible web manufacturer's directions. Before fusing traced mountain and land pieces to their chosen fabrics, trim away the excess fusible web in the center of each design, leaving about ¼" to ½" of fusible on the outer edges only to help reduce bulk.

3. Fuse designs to A as shown. Finish the raw edges as desired. Return A to the design wall.

4. Sew nine four-patch blocks following the checkerboard directions in Chapter 1. Use 2½"-wide strips. The blocks will measure 4½" square. From the sewn pairs of strips, cut 18 segments, each 2½" wide. Sew two segments together to make each four-patch unit.

5. Sew three four-patch units together, making a two square x six square checkerboard that measures 4½" x 12½".

Sew six four-patch units together, making a two square x 12 square checkerboard that measures 4½" x 24½". Place the checkerboard units on the design wall as shown in the Layout Diagram.

6. Sew the quilt top together in order, as shown in the Construction Diagram.

7. Quilt, embellish and bind the quilt as desired.

8. Add a hanging sleeve and label.

Cut

Fabric	Size	How Many	For
Light print	14" x 20"	2	Background
Dark print	14" x 20"	2	Border
Binding fabric	2½"-wide strips	4	Binding

Finished size: 12" x 18".

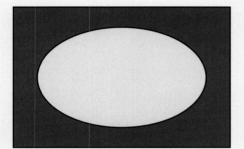

Chocolate Moose Place Mat
Layout Diagram

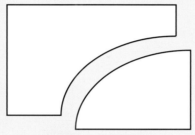

Chocolate Moose
Oval Cutting Diagram

You Will Need

(For Two Place Mats)

- 1 yd. dark print (border, binding)
- ½ yd. light fabric (background)
- ½ yd. fabric (backing)
- 1 dark fat quarter (moose)
- ⅛ yd. green fabric (branches, shrubs)
- 3" x 3" scraps in black and medium brown (geese, small moose)
- ½ yd. batting
- ¾ yd. fusible web
- Thread, plus decorative threads for embellishing and detailing
- Temporary spray adhesive (optional)
- Paper to create template
- Appliqué patterns:
  Fur 9, Fur 10, Fur 11, Fur 12, Fur 13, Fur 13A, Fur 14, Fur 15, Fur 16, Fur 17, Fur 18, Fur 19
- General sewing tools (Chapter 1)

Construction and Quilting

1. Fold the dark print fabric in half; press. Fold it in half again; press. Your border fabric is now folded into fourths.

2. Make a paper template from the oval pattern provided. Place the template on the folded fabric, aligning the 90-degree corner with the folded corner of fabric. The template curve will be near the raw edges of fabric. Trace around the curve. Pin the layers together; cut and remove the oval. Refer to the cutting diagram.

3. Open up the fabric. Sew a scant ¼" from the raw edge of the oval opening. Working from the wrong side of the fabric, use this stitching line as a guide to turn under the raw edge and form a finished edge with a gentle curve. Press.

4. Center the border piece on top of the background fabric. Align the raw edges and pin the layers together in a few places. Use the opening as a guide for design placement.

5. Trace and cut out the desired appliqués (moose, trees, birds, etc.); follow the fusible web manufacturer's directions. Trace five or six branch pieces (Fur 11 or Fur 12); cut the pieces apart and place them around the oval to form a pleasing frame. Some designs may extend out of view and below the oval frame. Fuse the appliqués in place once all of the items are in position. Finish the raw edges as desired.

6. Pin the oval opening in place. Sew down the curved edge of the oval by hand or machine; use a decorative stitch, topstitch, blanket stitch or invisible stitch.

7. Trim the place mat to 12½" x 18½". If desired, remove the excess background fabric.

8. Baste, quilt, embellish and bind the place mat as desired. See Chapter 1.

Tip
Use temporary spray adhesive to save time and effort when basting place mats.

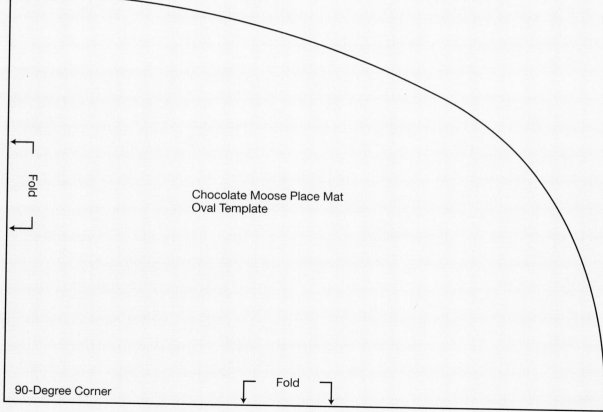

Fold

Chocolate Moose Place Mat
Oval Template

Fold

90-Degree Corner

Cut

From	Size	How Many	For
A	12½" x 14½"	2	Background
B	1½" x 42½"	2	Inner border
C	1½" x 16½"	2	Inner border
D	2½" x 44½"	2	Outer border
E	2½" x 20½"	2	Outer border
Light checkerboard	2½"-wide strips	3	Checkerboard
Medium checkerboard	2½"-wide strips	3	Checkerboard
Binding fabric	2½"-wide strips	4	Binding

Finished size: 20" x 48".

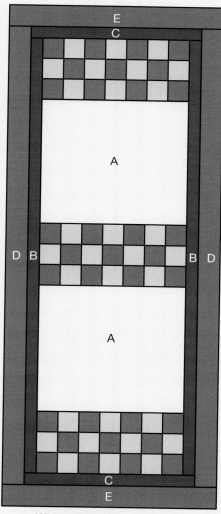

Whitetail Walk Table Runner
Layout Diagram

You Will Need

- ⅔ yd. medium fabric (outer border, checkerboards)
- ½ yd. dark fabric (inner border, binding)
- ½ yd. light fabric (background)
- ¼ yd. light fabric (checkerboards)
- 3 green fat quarters (1 light, 1 medium and 1 dark for mountains and land)
- 1 dark brown fat quarter (deer)
- ⅛ yd. dark brown fabric (tree trunk)
- Scraps of greens and dark brown or black (tree leaves, birds)
- 1½ yd. fabric (quilt back)
- ⅔ yd. batting, 50" or wider
- 1½ yd. fusible web
- Thread, plus decorative threads for embellishing and detailing
- Appliqué patterns:
  Fur 20, Fur 21, Fur 22, Fur 23, Fur 24, Fur 25, Fur 25A, Fur 26, Fur 27, Fur 28, Fur 29, Fur 43, Fur 44, Fur 45, Fur 46, Fur 46A, Fur 46B, Fur 46C
- General sewing tools (Chapter 1)

Notes: The yardage listed is for borders cut on cross grain and pieced as needed. For straight-of-grain cuts, purchase 1¼ yd. inner border and 1⅜ yd. outer border fabric.

The mountains have simple curves and easily can be hand appliquéd if you prefer; see Chapter 1. Suggested grainline markings on mountain pieces are for reference with directional prints.

To shorten or lengthen the table runner, adjust the number of checkerboards in the center area, and adjust your fabric amounts accordingly.

Construction and Quilting

1. Refer to the Layout Diagram to position each piece of the table runner on a design wall or other work surface.

2. Trace and cut out the appliqué designs; follow the fusible web manufacturer's directions. Tip: Before fusing the traced mountain and land pieces to their chosen fabrics, trim away the excess fusible in the center of each design, leaving ¼" to ½" on the outer edges only; this will reduce bulk.

3. Fuse the designs to A. Finish raw edges as desired. Return A to the design wall.

4. Sew checkerboards following directions in Chapter 1. Use a 2½"-wide strip. Sew two light and two medium strips together, alternating colors; this now measures 8½" wide. Sew the remaining pair of strips together; this now measures 4½" wide.

5. Cut each of these into as many 2½"-wide segments as possible.

6. Sew the 2½"-wide segments together, or remove stitching as needed to form nine checkerboard strips that are one square tall x nine squares wide. Of the strips, six should begin and end with medium fabric, and three should begin and end with light fabric.

7. Refer to the Layout Diagram to sew three checkerboard units that are three squares tall x nine squares wide.

8. Place the completed checkerboard units on the design wall.

9. Sew the checkerboard units to A pieces as shown in the Layout Diagram.

10. Add the borders in alphabetical order, pressing each seam away from the center. Piece borders if needed. Square up the runner after adding C. Square up the runner again after adding E.

11. Quilt, embellish and bind the runner as desired. See Chapter 1.

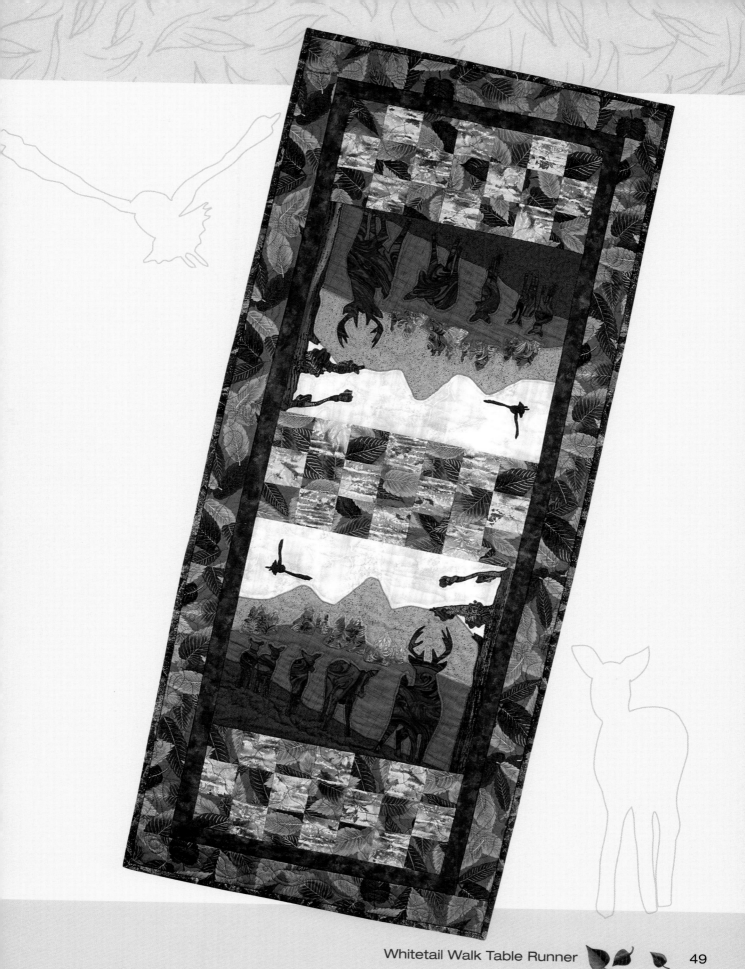

Whitetail Walk Bath Towel

 Fur

Finished towel size shown: 30" x 56".

You Will Need

- Purchased bath towel
- 1 dark fat quarter (deer)
- 2½"-wide light strip (checkerboard)
- 2½"-wide dark strip (checkerboard)
- ¼ yd. fusible web
- 10" x 20" tear-away stabilizer
- Thread
- Embroidery floss (optional)
- Appliqué patterns:
  Fur 21, Fur 22, Fur 23, Fur 25
- General sewing tools (Chapter 1)

Note: When selecting towels to use in this project, consider the fiber content, quality and nap.

Construction

1. Use 2½"-wide strips to sew checkerboard strips, following directions in Chapter 1.
2. Cut 15 segments, each 2½"-wide, from the sewn pair of strips.
3. Sew the segments together to make two checkerboard strips that are one square tall x 15 squares wide. You may need to add or subtract squares depending on the width of your towel. Press the seams all in one direction.
4. Stay stitch a scant ¼" from all edges of the checkerboard strips. Turn under raw edges along the stitching line; press.

5. Pin the checkerboard strips in place on the towel and topstitch. The towels shown had a band of tightly woven material near the ends; I placed the checkerboard strip on top of this.
6. Following the fusible web manufacturer's directions, trace and cut out one each of the following designs: Fur 21, Fur 22, Fur 23, Fur 25, reversed Fur 21, reversed Fur 22 and reversed Fur 23. See Chapter 1 for tips on reversing designs.
7. Position the deer designs on the towel as shown, and fuse or hand appliqué in place. Your fusible may not adhere completely to napped towels.
8. Anchor the design using your favorite method. Finish the raw edges of your fused designs as desired. The towel shown was free-motion stitched just inside the edge of each item and sewn through the deer, towel and stabilizer. The stabilizer was removed after stitching was completed. By hand, try a blanket stitch with three strands of embroidery floss. Press.

Tip

Some towels have a nap and don't work well with fusibles. I found that my fusible would adhere designs in place long enough for me to stitch through them by machine, but was too weak to leave designs unstitched.

Whitetail Walk Hand Towel

Finished hand towel size shown: 16" x 30".

Tip

Now that you've added a custom touch to a towel, how about decorating a bathroom shower curtain to match your theme? Or adding these designs to a pair of terry towel wraps — one for him, one for her. These versatile appliqués offer endless possibilities to decorate your neck of the woods.

Construction

Follow the directions for the Whitetail Walk Bath Towel, with changes to these steps:

1. Use 2"-wide strips.
2. Cut 11 segments, each 2" wide.
3. Make two checkerboard strips that measure one square tall x 11 squares wide (or to fit the width of your towel).
4. Following the fusible web manufacturer's directions, trace and cut out one each of the following designs: Fur 22, Fur 23, Fur 24, Fur 25 and reversed Fur 22. See Chapter 1 for tips on reversing designs.

You Will Need

- Purchased hand towel
- 1 fat quarter of dark fabric (deer)
- 2"-wide strip of light fabric (checkerboard)
- 2"-wide strip of dark fabric (checkerboard)
- 12" square of fusible web
- 9" x 14" piece of tear-away stabilizer
- Thread
- Appliqué patterns:
  Fur 22, Fur 23, Fur 24, Fur 25
- General sewing tools (Chapter 1)

Whitetail Walk Washcloth

Finished washcloth size shown: 12" x 12".

Construction

Follow the directions for the Whitetail Walk Bath Towel, with changes to these steps:

1. Use 2"-wide strips.
2. Cut five segments, each 2" wide.
3. Make a checkerboard strip of one square tall x nine squares wide, or to fit the width of your washcloth.
6. Trace and cut out four Fur 23 pieces.

You Will Need

- Purchased washcloth
- 7" x 7" dark fabric (deer)
- 2"-wide strip of light fabric (checkerboard)
- 2"-wide strip of dark fabric (checkerboard)
- 7" x 7" fusible web
- 6" x 12" tear-away stabilizer
- Thread
- Appliqué pattern: Fur 23
- General sewing tools (Chapter 1)

Bear's Paw Quilt

Cut

From	Size	How Many	For
A	5½" squares	16	Background behind bears
B	5½" squares	4	Background by bear toes
C	3" x 15½"	16	Inner borders
D	3" squares	16	Inner border corner squares
E	3½" x 40½"	2	Outer border
F	3½" x 46½"	2	Outer border
Light fabric	6" squares	8	Half-square triangles (bear toes)
Medium fabric	6" squares	8	Half-square triangles (bear toes)
Binding fabric	2½"-wide strips	5	Binding

Finished size: 46" square. Machine quilted by Aimee Simmons.

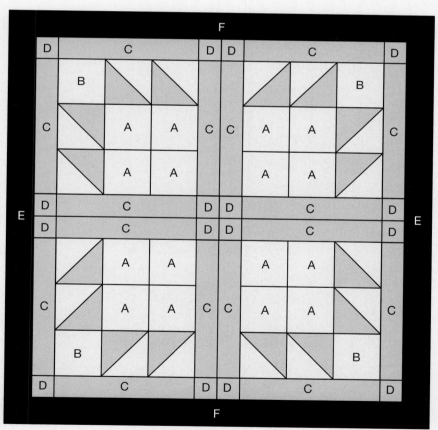

Bear's Paw Quilt Layout Diagram

You Will Need

- 1 yd.* dark fabric (outer border, binding)
- 1 yd. medium fabric (background behind bears, half-square triangles for bear paw shape)
- 1 yd. scrappy light fabrics (inner borders)
- ⅝ yd. light fabric (half-square triangles)
- ¼ yd. medium fabric (inner border contrasting squares)
- 1 dark fat quarter (bears)
- 12" x 12" dark fabric (trees)
- 12" x 12" brown fabric (tree trunks, snags)
- Scraps in pinks, greens, browns and yellows (clouds, grass, sun, moon)
- 2¾ yd. fabric (quilt back, hanging sleeve)
- 1½ yd. batting, at least 50" wide
- 1 yd. fusible web
- Thread
- Appliqué patterns: Fur 30, Fur 31, Fur 32, Fur 32A, Fur 33, Fur 33A, Fur 34, Fur 34R, Fur 35, Fur 35R, Fur 36, Fur 36R, Fur 37, Fur 47, Fur 48
- General sewing tools (Chapter 1)

*Note: Yardage listed is the amount needed for borders cut on the cross grain and pieced as needed. To cut borders and binding on the straight of grain, purchase 1½ yd. dark fabric.

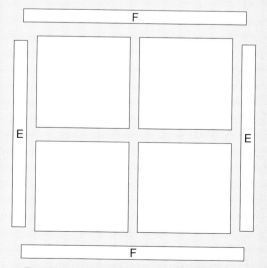

Bear's Paw Quilt Construction Diagram

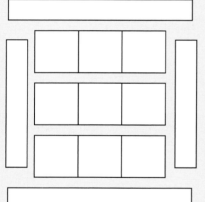

Framed Bear's Paw Block
Construction Diagram

D | C | D
C | B | | C
 | A | A
 | A | A
D | C | D

Framed Bear's Paw Block
Layout Diagram

Construction and Quilting

1. Refer to the Quilt Layout Diagram to position each piece of your wall hanging on a design wall or other work surface. For a scrappy look, experiment with fabric placement.

2. Make four framed bear's paw blocks, referring to the Block Layout Diagram and Construction Diagram. Directions follow.

3. Sew half-square triangles following directions in Chapter 1. Use 6" squares of light and medium fabric. Make 16 half-square triangles; trim each to 5½" square. Return the pieces to the design wall.

4. Sew each block together, row by row. Sew the rows together. Press all of the seams open.

5. Add side border C. Press the seams open or toward the border.

6. Sew one D to the ends of the remaining C pieces; add to the top and bottom of each paw block. Press the seams open or to the border. This completes the frame around each paw. Place the completed blocks on the design wall; pay close attention to block orientation.

7. Following the fusible web manufacturer's directions, trace and cut out two of each appliqué design Fur 30, Fur 31, Fur 32, Fur 33, Fur 34, Fur 35, Fur 36 and Fur 37 and two each of Fur 34R, Fur 35R and Fur 36R. Trace and cut out one or two each of Fur 47 and Fur 48.

8. Position and fuse the elements in place. Finish the raw edges as desired.

9. Refer to the Quilt Construction Diagram. Sew pairs of framed bear's paw blocks together. Sew the top row (two blocks) to the bottom row. Press the seams open.

10. Add borders D and then E. Press the seams open or toward the border.

11. Quilt, embellish and bind as desired.

12. Add a hanging sleeve and label.

Variation: Single Bear's Paw Wall Hanging

Cut

From	Size	How Many	For
A	5½" squares	4	Background behind bear
B	5½" squares	1	Background by bear toes
C	3" x 15½"	4	Outer border
D	3" squares	4	Outer border corner squares
Light fabric	6" squares	2	Half-square triangles (bear toes)
Medium fabric	6" squares	2	Half-square triangles (bear toes)
Binding fabric	2½"-wide strips	2	Binding

Finished size: 20" x 20".

Construction and Quilting

Follow the construction steps for the Bear's Paw Quilt with changes to these steps:

1. Refer to Single Bear's Paw Wall Hanging Layout Diagram.

2. Make one framed bear's paw block.

3. Make four half-square triangles.

9. Skip step.

10. Skip step.

You Will Need

- ¼ yd. dark fabric (outer border, binding)
- ¼ yd. scrappy medium fabrics (background behind bears, half-square triangles for bear paw shape)
- ¼ yd. scrappy light fabrics (half-square triangles for bear paw shape)
- ⅛ yd. light print (corner squares)
- 3" x 15" scrap of brown fabric (tree)
- 8" x 8" scrap of black fabric (bear)
- Scraps in pink, green and yellow (cloud, grass, sun/moon)
- ¾ yd. fabric (quilt back, hanging sleeve)
- ⅔ yd. batting, at least 20" wide
- ½ yd. fusible web
- Thread
- Appliqué patterns: Fur 30, Fur 34, Fur 35, Fur 36, Fur 37
- General sewing tools (Chapter 1)

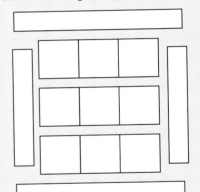

Single Bear's Paw Wall Hanging Construction Diagram

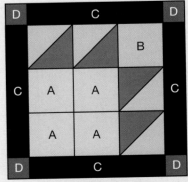

Single Bear's Paw Wall Hanging Layout Diagram

   Fur

Chapter 3
Fin

Fishing enthusiasts will love the projects grouped in this chapter, from a set of place mats and a matching table runner to coordinated napkins and coasters and a variety of wall hangings. There are plenty of designs to carry the fishing theme throughout your home. Your hardest decision will be which project to make first! Many of the fused designs are made into a unit, which makes alignment and placement simpler. This may be a new concept to you; if so, review the fusible tips and techniques in Chapter 1.

Cut

From	Size	How Many	For
A	5½" x 14½"	2	Sky
B	3½" x 14½"	2	Water
C	2½" x 8½"	4	Border
D	2½" x 18½"	4	Border
Binding fabric	2½"-wide strips	4	Binding

Finished size each: 12" x 18". Shown with coordinating napkins.

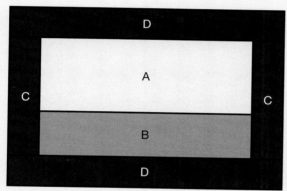

Fishing For An Invitation Place Mat Layout Diagram

You Will Need

(For Two Place Mats)

- ¾ yd. dark fabric (border, binding)
- 1 light fat quarter (sky)
- 1 light-medium fat quarter (water)
- 1 dark fat quarter (mountain)
- 1 medium fat quarter (mountain)
- 12" x 12" light-medium fabric (mountain)
- Scraps in black, black/brown print, silver or gray, dark gray print, green, blue and white (boat, rod and reel appliqués)
- ⅝ yd. fabric (backing)
- ½ yd. batting
- 1½ yd. fusible web
- Black thread plus decorative threads for embellishing and detailing
- Temporary spray adhesive (optional)
- Appliqué patterns: Fishing Reel B parts 1 through 6, Fin 1, Fin 2, Fin 3, Fin 4
- General sewing tools (Chapter 1)

Construction and Quilting

1. Refer to the Layout Diagram.
2. Trace one each of design elements Reel B parts 1 through 5 and Fin 4 (sails); trace four each of Reel B part 6; trace two each of Fin 1, Fin 2 and Fin 3 (mountains). For each fishing reel (the part that has the handle and spool of fishing line), create an appliqué unit using a nonstick pressing sheet (see Chapter 1). Refer to Layout Diagrams for each reel. The rod is a separate piece at this point.
3. Cut sails (Fin 4) from the bias edge of white fabric; this will reduce fraying. Optional: Make sails with stitching or embroidery.

4. Cut fabric for the fishing rod (the long, skinny part of fishing pole attached to the reel) with your rotary cutter, following these directions: Fuse a ⅜" x 12" strip of fusible web for each rod to its chosen fabric. Cut a ¼" strip from this fused fabric for each fishing pole.
5. Create the mountain designs. Before fusing the traced mountains to your chosen fabric, trim away the excess fusible in center of each large design, leaving about ¼" to ½" of fusible on outer edges only; this will reduce bulk.

6. Fuse the mountains to A as shown in photo. The mountains extend to the raw edges on the sides and bottom.

7. Sew A + B with an accurate ¼" seam; press the seam toward B.

8. Position the reel on the background, allowing for a seam allowance below. Add the rod; extend the tip of the rod to the raw edge of B, and tuck the other end under the reel unit. Keep the handle out of the seam. Fuse the piece in place. Finish the raw edges of the designs as you prefer.

9. Add C + D; press the seams toward the borders. Square up the piece to 12½" x 18½".

10. Baste, quilt, embellish and bind the place mat as desired. Add sails using a tiny bit of strong fusible web or fabric glue, or make sails with thread work only. Sew the fishing line from the spool up to the end of the rod; this can be done by hand or machine. Experiment with stitches on your machine, or try two lines of stitching. Or, sew the line by hand with a back stitch, running stitch or outline stitch.

Tip
Save time and effort by basting your place mats with temporary spray adhesive.

Cut

From	Size	How Many	For
A	6" x 15½"	2	Sky
B	4½" x 15½"	2	Water
C	3½" x 19½"	5	Center strips
D	3½" x 38½"	2	Border
E	3½" x 21½"	2	Border
Medium fabric	7" circle	1	Center circle
Dark or medium fabric	8" circle	1	Large center circle
Binding fabric	2½" strips	4	Binding

Note: A dinner plate may be the right size to use as a template for your circle(s). Use the same plate for both circles, and take a larger seam on one that will result in a smaller finished size.

Finished size: 21" x 44".

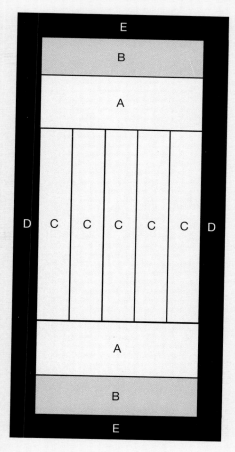

Fishing For An Invitation Table Runner
Layout Diagram

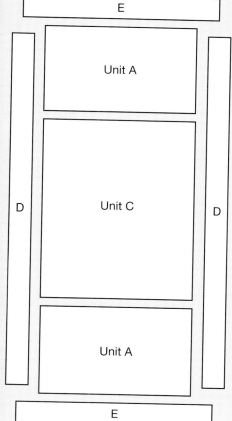

Fishing For An Invitation Table Runner
Construction Diagram

You Will Need:

- 1 yd. dark fabric (borders, binding)
- ½ yd. medium fabric (water, center circle)
- ½ yd. total of light fabric with at least a 40" usable width (center strips)
- 1 light fat quarter (sky)
- 1 dark fat quarter (mountain)
- 1 medium fat quarter (mountain)
- 12" x 12" light-medium square (mountain)
- Scraps of black, black/brown print, silver or gray, dark gray print, green, blue and white fabrics (appliqués)
- 1½ yd. fabric (quilt back)
- ¾ yd. batting, at least 50" wide
- 1½ yd. fusible web
- ¼ yd. lightweight, nonwoven interfacing
- Thread in black and white, plus decorative threads for embellishing and detailing
- Appliqué patterns: Reel A parts 1 through 5, Reel B parts 1 through 6, Fin 1, Fin 2, Fin 3, Fin 4
- General sewing tools (Chapter 1)

Note: To change the length of the table runner, adjust the length of pieces C and D, and adjust the fabric yardages accordingly.

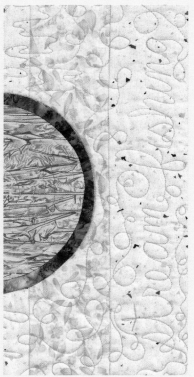

Construction and Quilting

1. Refer to the Layout and Construction Diagrams.
2. Follow Steps 2 through 8 for the Fishing For An Invitation Place Mat. Trace and cut the same designs, plus one each of Reel A parts 1 through 4 and four each of Reel A part 5.
3. Each section you just made with mountains and fishing poles is called A. Place A on the design wall.
4. Sew C strips together as desired; press the seams away from the center.
5. Sew A + C + A. Press the seams toward C.
6. Add D + E. Press the seams toward the borders.
7. Find the center of C. Appliqué or topstitch the larger circle first, then add the smaller one on top. My favorite method is to start by sewing a layer of lightweight interfacing right sides together to each circle. Next, cut a slit in the center of the interfacing only; turn the piece right side out and press. Trim away the center area of the interfacing to reduce bulk, then hand appliqué the design in place.
8. Quilt, embellish and bind the runner as desired. This project features quilted words related to fishing to add a special touch. Add sails and fishing line as described in Fishing For An Invitation Place Mat instructions.

Finished size: 12½" x 12½"

Construction

1. If you are using a purchased napkin, skip to Step 2. If you are sewing a napkin, finish the raw edges of your napkin square by folding all raw edges under approximately ¼". Press the edges; fold the edges under another ¼", and press again. Topstitch near the inner folded edge. Optional: You can use a special foot designed for your sewing machine that folds the fabric under as you stitch; this eliminates the pressing steps, but it takes some practice to make edges look professional.

2. Fuse the selected design to the right side of one corner of the napkin. Refer to Chapter 1 for fusible tips and techniques.

3. Anchor the design. If machine stitching the design, pin the stabilizer in place below the napkin and the fused design. Stitch through the design to finish the edge as desired. Remove the stabilizer. If you are hand stitching, use your favorite method, such as a blanket stitch with three strands of embroidery floss.

4. Press.

You Will Need

(For One Napkin)
- Purchased fabric napkin, or 13½" square of background fabric
- Scraps of gold, gray, small corn print and ruddy red (lures)
- Scraps of fusible web
- Decorative thread
- Scrap of tear-away stabilizer (for machine stitching)
- Appliqué patterns:
  Lure A parts 1 through 4, Lure D parts 13 and 14
- General sewing tools (Chapter 1)

Note: The napkins shown were made from a square of fabric. The lures were made as a unit and then fused in place with raw edges sewn down by machine using a stabilizer. If you would like to hand stitch the designs in place, you can swap embroidery thread for the decorative thread and skip the stabilizer.

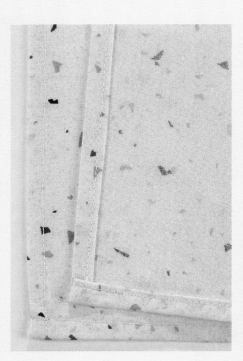

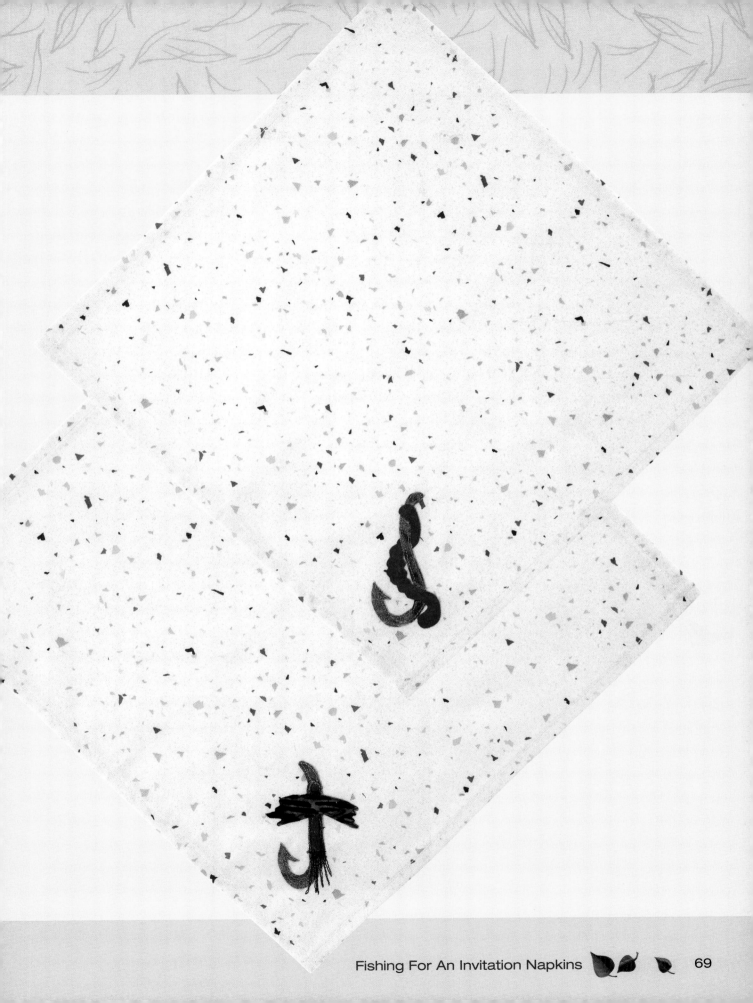

Finished size: 4" in diameter.

Construction

1. Attach the background fabric to one side of the stiff interfacing using either a sewable, fusible web or a glue stick.
2. Trim the background fabric even with the circle.
3. Repeat Steps 1 and 2 for the other side of the interfacing.
4. Fuse the selected design to one side of the coaster (see Chapter 1).
5. Quilt the coaster as desired. I prefer to sew through my design, about $\frac{1}{8}$" inside all edges, changing thread as needed. This anchors the design in place, quilts and adds some texture to the coaster all at the same time.
6. Use matching, contrasting or decorative thread to satin stitch around the raw edge of the coaster.

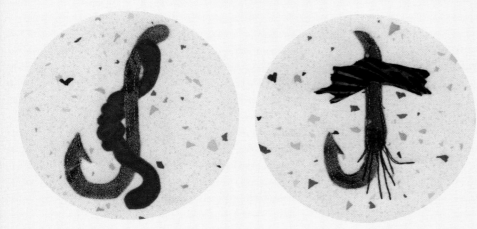

You Will Need

(For One Coaster)

- 1 circle, 4" in diameter, of stiff interfacing
- 2 squares, 4" x 4", of background fabric
- Scrap fabrics in gold, gray, small corn print and ruddy red (lures)
- Scraps of fusible web
- Glue stick (optional)
- Decorative thread, or thread to match/contrast the fabric
- Appliqué patterns:
  Lure A parts 1 through 4, Lure D parts 13 and 14
- General sewing tools (Chapter 1)

Note: These coasters are made with a single layer of Timtex (a stiff nonwoven interfacing), covered on each side with 100 percent cotton fabric. At this point they are embellished by fusing a design to one side and quilting through all layers. Timtex is completely washable and easy to sew through, yet retains its stiffness and shape after washing and handling. For more information, see Contributors.

Tip

I use these basic settings for a satin stitch: Stitch Length = 0.5; Stitch Width = 3.5. If edge still looks unfinished, repeat, using a wider stitch if possible. Having trouble holding on to your coaster? Get a grip on your circle by placing four long pins into the sides of the interfacing at the four compass positions (north, south, east and west), parallel to the table top. Hold these pins as you spin the circle and sew.

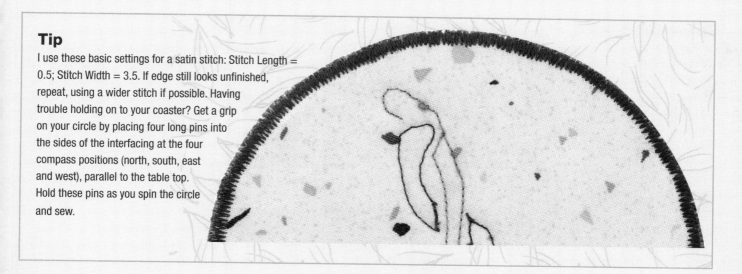

Fish Tale Wall Hanging

  Fin

Cut

From	Size	How Many	For
A	6" x 12½"	1	Sky
B	9" x 12½"	1	Water
C	1½" x 14½"	2	Inner border
D	1½" x 14½"	2	Inner border
E	2½" x 16½"	2	Middle border
F	2½" x 18½"	2	Middle border
G	4" x 20½"	2	Outer border
H	4" x 25½"	2	Outer border
Binding fabric	2½"-wide strips	3	Binding

Finished size: 25" x 27".

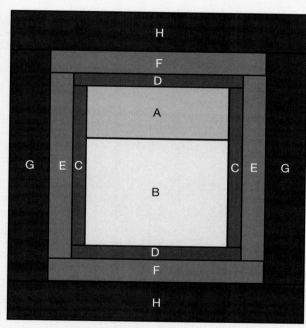

Fish Tale Wall Hanging Layout Diagram

You Will Need

- ⅞ yd. dark fabric (outer border, binding)
- ¼ yd. medium fabric (middle border)
- ⅛ yd. dark fabric (inner border)
- 1 light fat quarter (sky)
- 1 light fat quarter (water)
- 1 dark fat quarter (fish main color)
- ⅛ yd. medium-dark fabric (mountain)
- ⅛ yd. medium fabric (mountain's reflection)
- 12" x 12" black fabric (anglers, birds)
- Scraps in colors to contrast with fish (fish fins, eye, belly)
- 1 yd. fabric (quilt back, hanging sleeve)
- 1 yd. batting
- 1 yd. fusible web
- Fly or other fishing lure, with hook removed (optional)
- Thread in black, plus decorative threads for embellishing and detailing
- Appliqué patterns: Fish parts 1 through 10, Fin 5, Fin 6, Fin 7, Fin 8, Fin 9, Fin 10, Fin 11
- General sewing tools (Chapter 1)

Construction and Quilting

1. Refer to the Layout Diagram to position each piece of your wall hanging on a design wall or other work surface. Refer to the Construction Diagram as you prepare to sew.
2. Trace and cut out the design elements, one each, following the fusible web manufacturer's directions.
3. Create a fish unit using a nonstick pressing sheet (see Chapter 1). Use the Fish Layout Diagram to position the parts.
4. Place the mountain on A and mountain reflection on B, ⅛" from their respective raw edges. This will minimize bulk, with ⅛" of each fused design caught in the seam. Fuse.
5. Sew A + B with an accurate ¼" seam. Press the seam upward. Add the borders in alphabetical order, pressing each seam toward the border. Square up the piece after C and D are added and again after E and F and G and H.
6. Position the fish, anglers and birds. Fuse the pieces in place. Finish the appliqué raw edges as desired.
7. Quilt, embellish and bind the wall hanging as desired. For a three-dimensional touch, remove the hook from a fishing lure or fly and tack the piece in place. Quilt rings in the water below the fish to add a sense of movement.
8. Add a hanging sleeve and label (see Chapter 1).

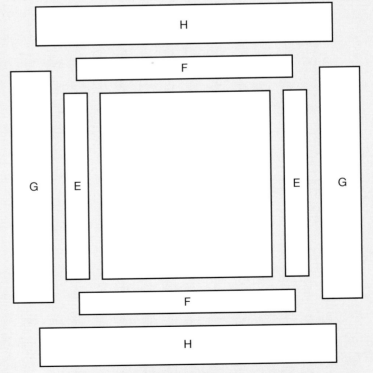

Fish Tale Wall Hanging Construction Diagram

Fin

Different fabric choices and three-dimensional touches, like a button eye and a real lure (bottom), can drastically alter the feel and look of a piece. Fabrics by P&B Textiles.

Cut

From	Size	How Many	For
Light fat quarter	15" square	1	Background
Dark fabric	15" square	1	Border
	2½"-wide strips	2	Binding

Finished size: 14" square.

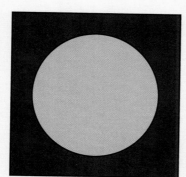

**Fish-In-A-Round Wall Hanging
Layout Diagram**

You Will Need

- ½ yd. dark fabric (border, binding)
- 1 light fat quarter (water/background)
- 1 dark fat quarter (main fish color)
- 1 fat quarter in desired color (quilt back, hanging sleeve)
- 1 fat quarter of batting
- Scraps of fabric in colors to contrast with fish (fish fins, eyes, belly)
- ½ yd. fusible web
- Decorative threads for embellishing and detailing
- Paper and pencil (to copy template)
- Temporary spray adhesive (optional)
- Appliqué patterns: Fish parts 1 through 10
- General sewing tools (Chapter 1)

Construction and Quilting

1. Fold the border fabric in half and press. Fold this in half again and press. Your border fabric now is folded into fourths.

2. Make a paper template from the Quarter Circle Template pattern. Place the paper template on folded fabric, aligning the 90-degree corner with the folded corner of fabric. The template curve will be near the raw edges of the fabric. Trace around the template. Pin the layers together, and cut the shape. Remove the circle.

3. Open up the fabric. Sew a scant ¼" from the raw edge around the circle opening. Working from the wrong side of the fabric, use this stitching line as a guide to turn under the raw edge and form a finished edge with a gentle curve. Press.

4. Place the border fabric on top of the background fabric; align the raw edges.

Pin the circle opening in place. Sew down the curved edge of the circle by hand or machine; use a topstitch, decorative stitch, blanket stitch or invisible stitch.

5. Trim the piece to 14½" square. Remove the excess background fabric, if desired.

6. Trace and cut out the design elements, one each, following the fusible web manufacturer's directions.

7. Create a fish unit using a nonstick pressing sheet as described in Chapter 1. Refer to the Fish Layout Diagram to position all parts.

8. Position and fuse the fish unit in place. Finish raw edges as desired.

9. Baste, quilt, embellish and bind as desired.

10. Add a hanging sleeve and label.

Cut

From	Size	How Many	For
A	18" x 24"	1	Background
D	4½" squares	4	Outer border corner squares
Dark fabric No. 1	3½" x 38"	1	Outer border
	3½" x 26"	2	Outer border
Dark fabric No. 2	1½" x 38"	1	Inner border
	1½" x 26"	2	Inner border
Binding fabric	2½" strips	3	Binding

Note: Borders are sewn with a speed technique that improves accuracy.

Finished size: 25½" x 27½". Shown with matching pillows.

Angler's Delight Wall Hanging
Layout Diagram

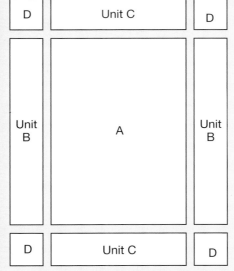

Angler's Delight Wall Hanging
Construction Diagram

You Will Need

- ½ yd. dark fabric No. 1 (outer border)
- ⅝ yd. dark fabric No. 2 (inner border and binding)
- ⅝ yd. light fabric (background)
- 1 or 2 fat quarters* (fishing rods)
- ⅛ yd. wood-grain print (rail fence)
- 12" x 12" black print (fish)
- 12" x 12" wicker print (creel)
- Scraps of dark brown, black/brown, silver or gray, dark gray, green, blue, gold, small corn print and ruddy red fabrics (appliqués)
- 1 yd. fabric (quilt back, hanging sleeve)
- 1 yd. batting
- 1½ yd. fusible web
- Thread in black and white, plus decorative threads for embellishing and detailing
- Slate gray embroidery floss; other colors optional
- Appliqué patterns:
  Fin 12, Fin 13, Fin 14, Fin 15, Fin 16, Fin 17, Fin 18, Reel A parts 1 through 5, Reel B parts 1 through 6, Wicker Creel parts 1 through 7, Net parts 1 and 2, Fly Rod, Spinning Rod, Lure A parts 1 through 4, Lure B parts 5 through 8, Lure C parts 9 through 12, Lure D parts 13 and 14
- General sewing tools (Chapter 1)

Note: If you choose to use the same fabric for both rods, you only need one fat quarter.

Construction and Quilting

1. Sew one outer border strip, 3½" x 26", to one inner border strip, 1½" x 26". Sew with an accurate ¼" seam; press the seams toward the outer border. Repeat.

2. Sew one outer border strip, 3½" x 38", to one inner border strip, 1½" x 38". Press the seam toward the outer border.

3. Verify that each pressed border unit measures 4½" wide. Make adjustments to the seams if needed.

4. Cut the border units as follows:

From	Size	How Many	For
26" lengths	24"-long unit	2	Unit B
38" length	18"-long unit	2	Unit C

5. Refer to the Layout Diagram to position each piece of your wall hanging on a design wall or other work surface. Make certain that the inner border on each border unit touches the background A piece. Refer to the Construction Diagram as you prepare to sew.

6. Sew Unit B + A + Unit B; press to Unit B.

7. Sew D + Unit C + D; press to Unit C. Repeat.

8. Sew the top and bottom rows to the center section. Press the seams toward the borders.

9. Trace and cut out each design element for this project, following fusible web manufacturer's directions. Use long-bladed scissors to cut fishing rods and fence pieces to get a cleaner finish. Trace and cut one of each design, with these exceptions: cut two Fin 13 fence post; cut six Reel A part 5; cut six Reel B part 6.

10. For each fishing reel (the part that has the handle and spool of fishing line), create a fusible unit using a nonstick pressing sheet as described in Chapter 1. Refer to the Layout Diagrams for each reel. Keep the rod separate at this point.

11. Follow the same fusible unit process for the rail fence, wicker creel, fishing net and lures.

12. Position all of the appliqué design pieces on the background. Begin by centering the rail fence about 4" from the lower edge of the background; add the wicker creel, and make adjustments. Place all of the other elements, making sure the curved rods cross in the center of the quilt top.

13. Follow the manufacturer's directions to fuse the elements in place. Finish the raw edges as desired.

14. Quilt and bind the wall hanging as desired. Add a hanging sleeve and label.

15. Embellish the piece by adding knotted colors of embroidery floss to the lures or in place of lures in the four corners. The fishing line on each piece as shown was sewn by machine in a thread matching each spool. A short length of embroidery floss attaches each hanging fish to the rail fence. Embellishing details can be done by hand embroidery with a back stitch, running stitch or outline stitch.

Tip
Give projects a custom look by trying different prints, color ways and embellishment techniques, such as with this blue and cream combination.

Cut

From	Size	How Many	For
A	10½" square	1	Background
B	2" x 10½"	2	Border
C	2" x 12½"	2	Border
Fabric of choice	13" square	1	Pillow back

Finished size: 12" square.

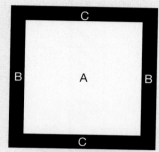

Angler's Delight Pillow
Layout Diagram

You Will Need

(For One Pillow)
- 1 light fat quarter (background)
- ⅛ yd. dark fabric (border)
- 1 coordinating fat quarter (pillow back)
- 12" x 12" black print (fish)
- 12" x 12" wicker print (creel)
- Scraps of dark brown (creel trim)
- ½ yd. fusible web
- 12" pillow form
- Thread
- Appliqué patterns:
  Wicker Creel parts 1 through 7,
  Fin 14
- General sewing tools (Chapter 1)

Construction

1. Refer to the Pillow Layout Diagram to position each piece of your pillow.
2. Sew pieces with an accurate ¼" seam in this order: A + B; AB + C. Press the seams toward the borders. Square up the piece to measure 12½" square.
3. Trace and cut out one each of the wicker creel elements and four Fin 14 pieces. Follow the fusible web manufacturer's directions.

4. Create a wicker creel unit using a nonstick pressing sheet as described in Chapter 1. Refer to the Wicker Creel Layout Diagram to position the parts as you make this unit.
5. Position the wicker creel and the fish on background as desired. Play with different placements of the fish — I've shown two versions, but there are many more. Fuse the pieces in place, and finish the raw edges of designs as desired.

6. Sew the pillow top right sides together to the pillow back, using a ⅜" seam. Leave an opening in the bottom approximately 9" to 10" wide. Turn the piece right side out. Press.
7. Insert the pillow form.
8. Whipstitch the opening closed.

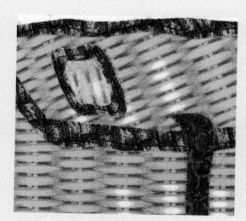

Fin

Birds of all kinds are abundant in the forest, though at first glance you may not notice them. I've captured some of my favorites in this chapter's projects. Why not start with the Wild Wings Table Runner and matching place mats, or the Feathered Friends Wall Hanging and coordinating Swan Lake Pillow? The Freedom's Flight Wall Hanging features an Americana theme, and a coordinating potholder is a snap to make. Several of these projects start by creating a single fused design unit by using a nonstick pressing sheet. If this is new to you, follow the step-by-step instructions in Chapter 1. Have fun embellishing and experimenting with threads as you add detail and life to each project.

Chapter 4
Feather

Wild Wings Table Runner

  Feather

Cut

From	Size	How Many	For
A	8½" x 14½"	2	Water
B	1½" x 14½"	2	Land
C	3½" x 14½"	2	Sky
D	2½" x 12½"	4	Border
E	2½" x 18½"	4	Border
F	2½" x 16½"	2	Border
G	4½" x 16½"	2	Center of runner, medium
H	6½" x 16½"	1	Center of runner, dark
Binding fabric	2½"-wide strips	4	Binding

Note: To shorten or lengthen the table runner, adjust the lengths of pieces F, G and H.

Finished size: 18" x 48".

You Will Need

- ¾ yd. dark fabric (borders, binding)
- ¼ yd. medium fabric (center of runner)
- ¼ yd. dark fabric (center of runner)
- ½ yd. medium fabric (water)
- ⅓ yd. various white fabrics or white-on-white prints (swan)
- Light fat quarter (sky)
- Medium-dark green fat quarter (grass, cattails)
- ⅛ yd. medium fabric (land)
- Scraps of yellow and brown (swan's bill, cattails)
- 1½ yd. coordinating fabric (quilt back)
- ⅝ yd. batting, 50" wide or greater
- 1½ yd. fusible web
- Thread in black and white, plus decorative threads for embellishing and detailing
- Appliqué patterns: Swan 1 parts 1 through 5, Swan 2 parts 6 through 10, Feather 2, Feather 2A, Feather 2B, Feather 2C, Feather 2D, Feather 3, Feather 3A, Feather 3B, Feather 3C
- General sewing tools (Chapter 1)

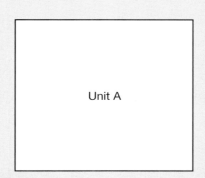

Wild Wings Table Runner
Layout Diagram

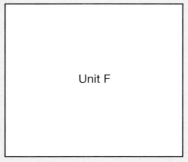

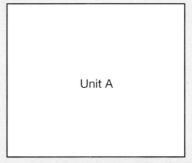

Wild Wings Table Runner
Construction Diagram

Construction and Quilting

1. Refer to the Layout Diagram to position each piece of your wall hanging on a design wall or other work surface. Refer to the Construction Diagram as you prepare to sew.

2. Sew with an accurate ¼" seam in alphabetical order: A + B; AB + C; ABC + D, ABCD + E. Press the seams toward the outer border. Square up the piece; it should measure 16½" x 18½"; this is Unit A. Repeat to make two identical units.

3. Sew F + G + H + G + F. Press the seams away from the center. This is Unit F.

4. Sew Unit A + Unit F + Unit A. Position the water near the outer ends of the table runner, as shown in the photo.

5. Trace and cut out elements of each swan and all of the other design pieces for the project. Follow the fusible web manufacturer's directions.

6. Create a unit for each swan, using a nonstick pressing sheet as described in Chapter 1. Use the Swan 1 and Swan 2 Layout Diagrams to position the swan parts.

7. Position the swan units and other design elements on the pieced background. Fuse the elements in place. Finish the raw edges of the appliqués as desired.

8. Quilt, embellish and bind the table runner as desired.

Tip

Each swan has black stitching on its face to form a line between the beak and head and to define the eye and nostril. You could use a permanent marking pen to color the black area on each swan's face rather than stitching. Thread work defines the feathers on the wings of the swans and anchors down all fused pieces. All of this is done with a free-motion stitch as part of the quilting process.

Wild Wings Place Mats

Cut

From	Size	How Many	For
A	8½" x 14½"	2	Sky
B	4½" x 14½"	2	Water
Dark fabric	5¼" squares	3	Flying geese
Light fabric	2⅞" squares	12	Flying geese
Binding fabric	2½"-wide strips	4	Binding

Finished size: 12" x 18".

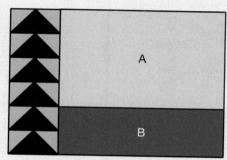

Wild Wings Place Mat Layout Diagram

You Will Need

(For Two Place Mats)

- ½ yd. dark fabric (flying geese, binding)
- ⅛ yd. light fabric (flying geese)
- Light fat quarter (sky)
- Medium fat quarter (water)
- Scraps of black, near-black print, gray, white and orange fabrics (bird appliqués)
- ½ yd. coordinating fabric (backing)
- ½ yd. batting
- ½ yd. fusible web
- Thread in black, plus decorative threads for embellishing and detailing
- Temporary spray adhesive (optional)
- Appliqué patterns:
  Feather 1, Goose 2 parts 1 through 8
- General sewing tools (Chapter 1)

Construction and Quilting

1. Follow the instructions for Fast Flying Geese given in Chapter 1. Make 12 flying geese, using light and dark squares. The unfinished size of each is 2½" x 4½".
2. Refer to the Wild Wings Place Mat Layout Diagram to position each piece of the place mat.
3. Sew together a stack of six flying geese; press the seams upward. Repeat.
4. Sew A + B. Press the seam toward B or open. Repeat.
5. Sew one flying geese stack to each AB unit, matching seams as appropriate.
6. Trace and cut out your choice of birds, following the fusible web manufacturer's directions. For the goose, create a unit using a nonstick pressing sheet as described in Chapter 1. Refer to the Goose 2 Layout Diagram.
7. Fuse the birds to the pieced background. Finish the raw edges as desired.
8. Baste, quilt, embellish and bind the place mats as desired.

Wild Wings Potholder

  Feather

Cut

From	Size	How Many	For
Background fabric	7" square	1	Background
Backing fabric	7" square	1	Backing
Cotton batting	7" square	1	Batting layer
Insulated batting	7" square	1	Insulating layer
Binding fabric	2½"-wide strip	1	Binding

Finished size: 6" square.

Construction

1. Fuse your chosen design to the right side of the background fabric piece. This is the quilt top.

2. Place the potholder top right side up on the cotton batting. Quilt as desired. Trim the batting to align with the quilt top. This is now the quilted top.

3. Make a quilt sandwich: quilted top right side up + insulated batting + potholder back wrong side up. Quilt as desired. Trim to 6¼" square.

4. Sew around the outer edges of the sandwich through all layers, using a ⅜" seam allowance.

5. Bind the potholder as you would a quilt, except that the beginning point is where the hanging loop will be. Choose the upper right or left corner of the potholder for the loop, so the design hangs right side up. Sew by machine as usual, extending the tail of the binding 3" beyond the overlap. Turn the binding over the raw edges and sew it down by hand. Fold the binding tail so there are no raw edges, and topstitch the binding along the length. Make a loop with the binding, and sew it down with a zigzag stitch.

You Will Need

(For One Potholder)
- 7" x 7" water or sky fabric (background)
- 7" x 7" coordinating fabric (backing)
- 7" x 7" cotton batting
- 7" x 7" specialty insulated batting
- Scraps of black, near-black print, gray, white, and orange (appliqué)
- Scraps of fusible web
- Decorative thread
- Purchased bias tape or ⅛ yd. coordinating fabric for binding
- Appliqué patterns: Goose 2 parts 1 through 8
- General sewing tools (Chapter 1)

Feathered Friends Wall Hanging

Cut

From	Size	How Many	For
A	8½" x 14½"	1	Water
B	1½" x 14½"	1	Land (shrubs, grass)
C	3½" x 14½"	1	Sky No. 1
D	4½" x 12½"	1	Sky No. 2
E	5½" x 18½"	1	Sky No. 3
F (green print No. 1)*	2" x 17½"	1	Inner border, light
F (green print No. 2)*	2" x 17½"	1	Inner border, medium
G (green print No. 1)*	2" x 21½"	1	Inner border, light
G (green print No. 2)*	2" x 21½"	1	Inner border, medium
H	3½" x 20½"	2	Outer border
I	3½" x 27½"	2	Outer border
Binding fabric	2½"-wide strips	3	Binding

*Note: If desired, you can use a single green fabric for the inner border. Cut the pieces to the same dimensions.

Finished size: 26" x 27".

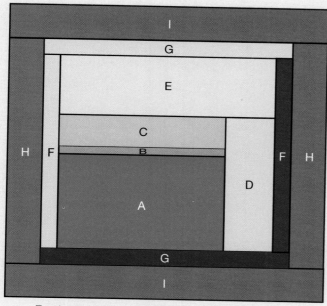

Feathered Friends Wall Hanging Layout Diagram

You Will Need

- ¾ yd. dark fabric (outer border, binding)
- ⅛ yd. light green print (inner border, fabric No. 1)
- ⅛ yd. medium green print (inner border, fabric No. 2)
- 1 medium fat quarter (water)
- 3 different medium sky-print fat quarters (sky; may have excess)
- ⅛ yd. medium fabric (land)
- ¼ yd. various whites or white-on-white prints (swans)
- ¼ yd. medium dark green print (grass and cattails)
- Scraps of yellow, orange, brown, black, near-black print and gray (bird and cattail appliqués)
- 1 yd. coordinating fabric (quilt back, hanging sleeve)
- 1 yd. batting
- 1½ yd. fusible web
- Thread in black and white, plus decorative threads for embellishing and detailing
- Appliqué patterns:
  Swan 1 parts 1 through 5, Swan 2 parts 6 through 10, Goose 1 parts 1 through 6, Goose 2 parts 1 through 8, Goose 3 parts 1 through 8, Goose 4 parts 1 through 8, Feather 1, Feather 2, Feather 2A, Feather 2B, Feather 2C, Feather 2D, Feather 3, Feather 3A, Feather 3B, Feather 3C, Feather 6, Feather 6A, Feather 7, Feather 7A, Feather 7B
- General sewing tools (Chapter 1)

Construction and Quilting

1. Refer to the Layout Diagram to position each piece of your wall hanging on a design wall or other work surface. Refer to the Construction Diagram as you prepare to sew.
2. Sew with accurate ¼" seam in alphabetical order: A + B; AB + C. Press the seams open or toward the water fabric. Sew ABC + D, ABCD + E. Press the seams toward D and E. Square up the piece; it should measure 17½" tall x 18½" wide. This unit is the center square area you see in the construction diagram.
3. Add borders F and G using two different prints as shown. If you prefer, use only one print. Sew the darker green print No. 2 to the right side and bottom; sew the lighter green print No. 1 to the left side and top. Press the seams toward the border. You may prefer to position your swans and grass at the bottom of your wall hanging before adding border G. Some pieces may need to be pinned out of the way as you sew those seams.
4. Add outer borders H and I. Press the seams toward the outer border.
5. Trace and cut out elements of each swan, each goose, the heron, the grass and the cattails. Follow the fusible web manufacturer's directions.
6. Create a unit with each swan, using a nonstick pressing sheet as described in Chapter 1. Refer to the Swan Layout Diagrams to position the parts. Repeat this process for each goose, using the Goose Layout Diagrams.
7. Position the swan units and geese units on the pieced background. Add the remaining design elements, with the heron, grass and cattails added last. Fuse the pieces in place. Finish the raw edges as desired.
8. Quilt, embellish and bind the wall hanging as desired. Use thread work to define the birds' wings and feathers, and the swan's eyes and bills. If desired, use a permanent marking pen to color, rather than stitch, the black area on each swan's face.
9. Add a hanging sleeve and label.

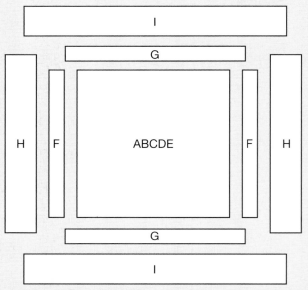

Feathered Friends Wall Hanging Construction Diagram

Swan Lake Pillow

  Feather

Cut

From	Size	How Many	For
A	8½" x 12½"	1	Water
B	1½" x 12½"	1	Land
C	3½" x 12½"	1	Sky
D	2½" x 12½"	2	Border
E	2½" x 16½"	2	Border
Fabric of choice	17" square	1	Pillow back

Finished size: 16" square.

Construction

1. Refer to the Layout Diagram to position each piece of your pillow.

2. Sew with accurate ¼" seam in alphabetical order: A + B; AB + C. Press the seams open or toward the water. Add borders D and E, pressing the seams toward the borders. Square up the piece; this should measure 16½" square.

3. Trace and cut out elements of each swan. Follow the fusible web manufacturer's directions.

4. Create a unit for each swan, as described in Wild Wings Table Runner project, Step 6. See Chapter 1 for additional information about fusibles.

5. Fuse swan units to the pieced background. Finish the raw edges as desired.

6. Layer the pillow top with cotton batting. If desired, place tear-away stabilizer below the batting. Quilt and embellish the pillow top as desired. Trim the batting even with the pillow top, and trim away excess stabilizer.

7. Use a ⅜" seam to sew the pillow top right sides together to pillow back. Leave an opening in the bottom approximately 12" to 13" wide. Turn the piece right side out. Press.

8. Insert the pillow form.

9. Whipstitch the pillow opening closed.

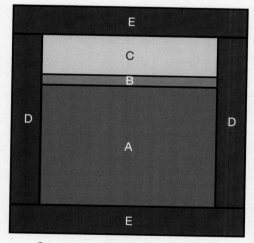

Swan Lake Pillow Layout Diagram

You Will Need

(For One Pillow)

- ¼ yd. dark fabric (border)
- 1 medium fat quarter (water)
- 1 light fat quarter (sky; may have some excess)
- ¼ yd. various whites or white-on-white prints (swans)
- ⅛ yd. medium green print (land)
- Scrap of yellow (swan bills)
- Coordinating fat quarter (pillow back)
- ½ yd. cotton batting (at least 18" wide)
- ¾ yd. fusible web
- ½ yd. tear-away stabilizer
- 16" pillow form
- Thread in black and white, plus decorative threads for embellishing and detailing
- Appliqué patterns: Swan 1 parts 1 through 5, Swan 2 parts 6 through 10
- General sewing tools (Chapter 1)

Freedom's Flight Wall Hanging

Cut

From	Size	How Many	For
A	2" x 15½"	3	Red stripes
B	2¾" x 15½"	1	Red stripe
C	2" x 15½"	2	Off-white stripes
D	2¾" x 15½"	1	Off-white stripe
E	3½" x 6½"	1	Blue background
F	2½" x 18½"	2	Inner border
G	2½" x 19½"	2	Inner border
H	4" x 22½"	2	Outer border
I	4" x 26½"	2	Outer border
Off-white fabric	1½" squares	8	Star blocks
	2" squares	16	Star blocks
Blue fabric	1½" squares	32	Star background
	2" squares	16	Star background
Binding fabric	2½"-wide strips	3	Binding

Finished size: 26" x 29". Fabrics by P&B Textiles.

You Will Need

- ¾ yd. blue print (outer border, binding)
- ¼ yd. red stripe (inner border)
- ⅓ yd. off-white stripe or print (center stripes, stars)
- ¼ yd. red print (center stripes)
- ¼ yd. blue print (star background)
- ¼ yd. various brown wood-grain prints (eagle body, wings)
- 12" x 12" white solid or white-on-white print (head, tail)
- Scraps of tan, gold or yellow (beak, talons)
- 1 yd. coordinating fabric (quilt back, hanging sleeve)
- 1 yd. batting
- 1½ yd. fusible web
- Black permanent pen, size 01
- Thread in black, white and brown, plus decorative threads for embellishing and detailing
- Appliqué patterns: Eagle parts 1 through 10
- General sewing tools (Chapter 1)

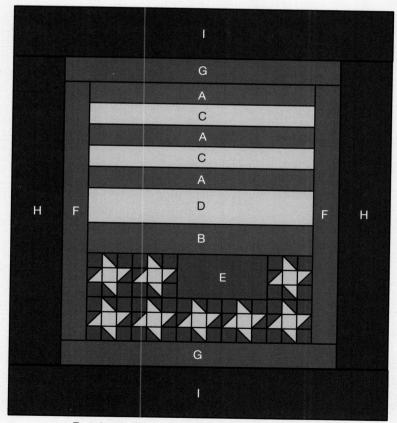

Freedom's Flight Wall Hanging Layout Diagram

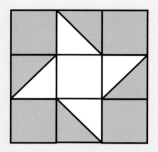

Star Block Layout Diagram

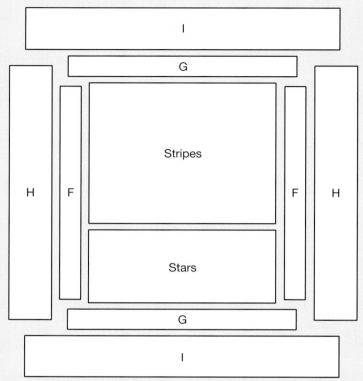

Freedom's Flight Wall Hanging Construction Diagram

In the construction diagram the labels read: I (top), G, H, F, Stripes, F, H, Stars, G, I (bottom).

Tip

The eye, nostril, and talons are drawn, traced, or colored in with black permanent pen; or, they can be stitched with black thread. Thread work defines the feathers on the eagle's tail and face, and it anchors down all fused pieces. This is done with a free-motion stitch as part of the quilting process.

Construction and Quilting

1. Refer to the Layout Diagram to position each piece of your wall hanging on a design wall or other work surface. Refer to the Construction Diagram as you prepare to sew.

2. Sew with accurate ¼" seam: A + C + A + C + A + D + B; press seams upward. This is the "stripes" section shown in the Construction Diagram; it should measure 12½" x 15½".

3. Make eight star blocks. Refer to Star Block Layout Diagram, and follow instructions for half-square triangles detailed in Chapter 1. Make 32 half-square triangles using 2" squares of off-white and blue; each should measure 1½" square unfinished. Sew each star block together in rows, just as you would for a nine-patch block. Press the seams open. The completed star blocks should measure 3½" square unfinished.

4. Sew two star blocks + E + one star block to form a row. Press open the seam between stars; press the other seams toward E. This should measure 15½" wide.

5. Sew five star blocks together in a row. Press open the seams between the stars. This piece should measure 15½" wide.

6. Sew star rows from Steps 4 and 5 together; press the seam open. This is the "stars" section shown in the Construction Diagram; it should measure 6½" x 15½".

7. Sew the Stripes to the Stars. Press the seam upward. Square up the piece; it should measure 15½" x 18½".

8. Add inner borders F and G; press the seams toward the border. Square up the piece. Add outer borders H and I; press the seams toward the border.

9. Before adding the eagle, baste, quilt and bind this base of the quilt. Do only minimal quilting; this simplifies the quilting process, and you will have fewer starts and stops. Do not quilt in E, the blank blue area in the center of the stars. Be aware that some of the quilting lines may show through the eagle when it is in place.

10. Trace and cut out elements of the eagle appliqué. Follow the fusible web manufacturer's directions.

11. Create an eagle unit using a nonstick pressing sheet as described in Chapter 1. Use the Layout Diagram to position the eagle parts.

12. Fuse the eagle unit to the pieced and quilted background. Finish the raw edges as desired.

13. Finish the detailed quilting. Embellish the quilt as desired.

14. Add a hanging sleeve and label.

Freedom's Flight Potholder

Finished size: 6" x 6".

Follow the instructions for the Wild Wings Potholder, except trace a star appliqué instead of a bird. Adjust your thread and fabric choices to get the look you desire.

Chapter 5
Flora

Bring a botanical touch to your home with projects that feature flowers and leaves. The flower projects are a perfect size to practice your machine thread work and to experiment with embellishing. They are made using a technique that fuses many small pieces into a single, movable, design unit. Refer to Chapter 1 for step-by-step instructions to learn how to create these units. A wall hanging, table runner, place mats, napkins, coasters and potholder that feature tree and leaf motifs round out the chapter; let your fabric choices determine which season they depict.

Cut

From	Size	How Many	For
1	5½" x 18"	3	Background
2	2½" x 18"	2	Inner border
3	2" x 18"	2	Inner border
C	2½" x 22½"	1	Inner border
D	2" x 22½"	2	Inner border
E	4" x 20½"	2	Outer border
F	4" x 29½"	2	Outer border
Binding fabric	2½"-wide strips	4	Binding

Finished size: 27" x 29".

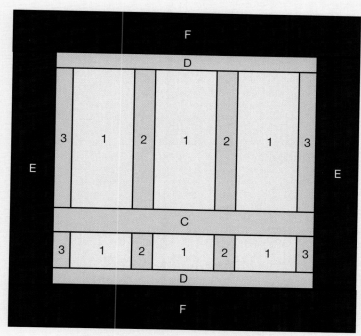

Turning Leaf Wall Hanging Layout Diagram

You Will Need

- 1 yd. dark print (outer border, binding)
- ⅜ yd. medium solid (inner border)
- ⅜ yd. light print (background)
- 1 yd. coordinating fabric (quilt back, hanging sleeve)
- 1 yd. batting
- 1 yd. fusible web
- 3 different 12" x 12" green prints (trees)
- Scraps of various greens or autumn colors (leaves)
- Scraps of brown (tree trunks)
- Decorative threads for embellishing, detailing and quilting
- Appliqué patterns:
  Tree 1, Tree 1A, Tree 2, Tree 2A, Tree 3, Tree 3A, Leaf 1, Leaf 2, Leaf 6, Leaf 7
- General sewing tools (Chapter 1)

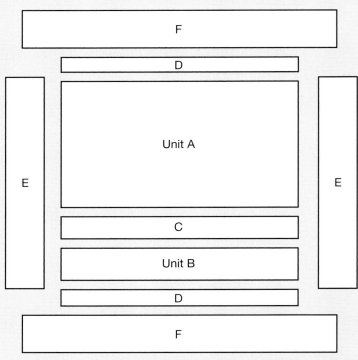

Turning Leaf Wall Hanging Construction Diagram

Tip

Stitch partial trunks and branches on each tree. Add birds or animals cut from novelty prints; add charms or buttons. Use the leaf patterns as templates to create detailed quilting designs in your border. Create more visual interest in quilting and other thread work by using variegated threads or specialty threads.

Construction and Quilting

1. Sew Units A and B. You will be sewing together the numbered 18" strips you cut for these units, making a large chunk of fabric. After pressing, Unit A and Unit B will be cut to exact size. This makes sewing easier and more accurate.

2. Arrange strips in this order (listed by their number in Cut directions): 3 + 1 + 2 + 1 + 2 + 1 + 3. See the Layout Diagram.

3. Use an accurate ¼" seam to sew the strips together along the length. Press the seams toward the borders. This is called a strata. Verify that the sewn piece measures 22½" wide. If not, make adjustments to seams to reach this width.

4. From strata, cut Unit A: 12½" x 22½".

5. From strata, cut Unit B: 3½" x 22½".

6. Refer to the Construction Diagram to position each piece of your wall hanging as you prepare to sew.

7. Sew D + Unit A + C + Unit B + D. Press the seams toward the borders.

8. Add E and F. Press the seams toward the outer borders.

9. Following the manufacturer's directions, cut and fuse the trees and leaves in place as shown. Cut two Leaf 6, cut three Leaf 7 and cut one of all of the other appliqué designs. Trees and leaves may extend into the inner borders. Finish the raw edges of the designs as desired.

10. Baste, quilt, embellish and bind the wall hanging as desired.

11. Add a hanging sleeve and label.

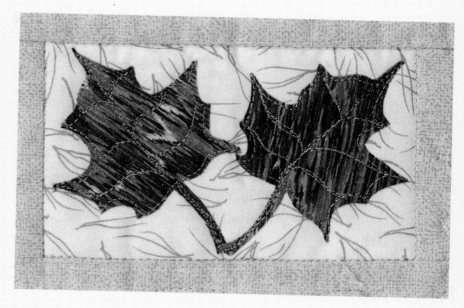

Turning Leaf Table Runner

Cut

From	Size	How Many	For
A	10½" square	2	Background
B	1½" x 10½"	4	Inner border
C	1½" x 12½"	4	Inner border
D*	3½" x 12½"	10	Outer border
E*	3½" square	8	Corner squares
F*	12½" square	1	Print (center of runner)
Binding fabric	2½"-wide strips	4	Binding

*Note: To shorten or lengthen the table runner, adjust the length of the pieces that make up unit F.

Finished size: 18" x 48".

You Will Need

- ⅞ yd. dark print (outer border, binding)
- ⅜ yd. any value of fabric (center of table runner, posts)
- ⅓ yd. light print (background)
- ¼ yd. medium solid (inner border)
- 1½ yd. coordinating fabric (quilt back)
- ⅝ yd. batting, at least 50" wide
- ¾ yd. fusible web
- 2 different 12" x 12" green prints (trees)
- Scraps of brown (trunks)
- Scraps of various green or autumn colors (leaves)
- Decorative thread for embellishing, detailing and quilting
- Appliqué patterns:
  Tree 3, Tree 3A
- General sewing tools (Chapter 1)

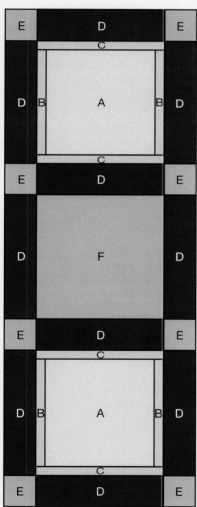

Turning Leaf Table Runner
Layout Diagram

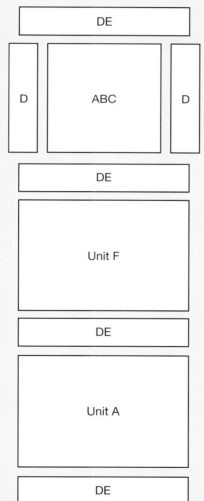

← Breakout View of Unit A

Turning Leaf Table Runner
Construction Diagram

Construction and Quilting

1. Refer to the Layout Diagram to position each piece of your table runner on a design wall or other work surface. Refer to the Construction Diagram as you prepare to sew.

2. Sew A + B + C using an accurate ¼" seam; press the seams away from A. Repeat, making a total of two identical units. Call each ABC.

3. Add D to each side of ABC. Press the seams toward D. Square up each piece; each one should measure 18½" wide. Make adjustments to the seams if needed. Call each Unit A.

4. Sew E + D + E, pressing the seams toward D. Repeat, making a total of four identical units. Each unit should measure 18½" wide. Call each DE.

5. Sew D + F + D, pressing the seams toward D. Square up the piece; it should measure 18½" wide. Call this Unit F.

6. Refer to the Construction Diagram to position all units. Sew the units together in rows, beginning at the top. Press the seams toward DE.

7. Trace and cut two tree motifs. Fuse the motifs in place as shown, following the manufacturer's directions. If desired, add leaves.

8. Quilt, embellish and bind the table runner as desired. Refer to the Turning Leaf Wall Hanging for tips on quilting and embellishing.

Turning Leaf Place Mats

  Flora

Cut

From	Size	How Many	For
A	4½" x 8½"	3	Background
B	1½" x 8½"	2	Border
C	2½" x 8½"	2	Border
D	2½" x 18½"	2	Border
Binding fabric	2½"-wide strips	2	Binding

Note: If you plan to make a set of place mats, refer to the construction directions for the Turning Leaf Wall Hanging, Steps 1, 2 and 3 for another piecing method. Instead of 8½" lengths for each place mat piece (A, B and C), cut them 18" long for two place mats); 27" for three place mats; or 36" for four place mats. The number of A, B and C pieces cut remains the same. Cut two D pieces for each place mat.

Finished size: 12" x 18".

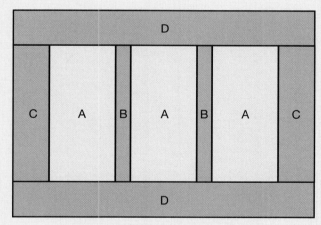

Turning Leaf Place Mat Layout Diagram

Construction and Quilting

1. Refer to the Layout Diagram to position each piece of your place mat.
2. Using an accurate ¼" seam, sew the following unit: C + A + B + A + B + A + C. Press the seams toward the borders.
3. Add D pieces. Press the seams toward D.
4. Following the fusible web manufacturer's directions, cut and fuse the leaves in place as shown. Finish the raw edges as desired.
5. Baste, quilt, embellish and bind the place mat as desired. Refer to the Turning Leaf Wall Hanging for tips on quilting and embellishing.

You Will Need

(For One Place Mat)
- ⅛ yd. medium or dark print (border)
- ⅛ yd. light print (background)
- ⅛ yd. dark print (binding)
- 1 coordinating fat quarter (place mat backing)
- 1 fat quarter of batting
- ⅛ yd. fusible web
- Scraps of various leaf-colored fabrics (leaves)
- Decorative threads for embellishing and detailing
- Temporary spray adhesive (optional)
- Appliqué patterns:
  Leaf 2, Leaf 3 and Leaf 4; or Leaf 5, Leaf 6 and Leaf 7
- General sewing tools (Chapter 1)

Tip
Consider using temporary spray adhesive to baste your place mats, which will save you time and effort.

Flora

Turning Leaf Napkins

Finished size: 12½" x 12½".

Follow the directions for the Fishing For An Invitation Napkins, except use the leaf appliqué patterns. Alter your thread and fabric choices to get the look you desire. The napkins shown were made from a square of fabric.

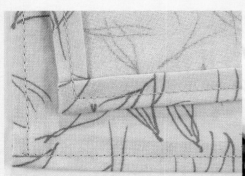

Turning Leaf Coasters

Finished size: 4" in diameter.

Follow the instructions for the Fishing For An Invitation Coasters, except use the leaf appliqué patterns instead. Adjust your thread and fabric choices to get the look you desire.

Turning Leaf Potholder

Finished size: 6¼" in diameter.

Follow the instructions for the Northern Exposure Potholders, except use a leaf appliqué pattern instead. Adjust your thread and fabric choices to get the look you desire.

Cut

From	Size	How Many	For
A	8½" square	1	Background
B	1½" x 8½"	2	Inner border
C	1½" x 10½"	2	Inner border
D	3½" x 10½"	2	Outer border
E	3½" x 16½"	2	Outer border
Binding fabric	2½"-wide strips	2	Binding

Finished size of each wall hanging: 16" x 16".

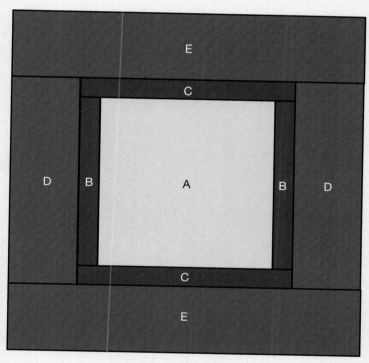

Precious Petals Trilogy Layout Diagram

You Will Need

(For One Wall Hanging)

- ⅜ yd. medium or dark print (outer border, binding)
- ⅛ yd. dark solid (inner border)
- 9" x 9" light fabric (background)
- 1 coordinating fat quarter (quilt back, hanging sleeve)
- 18" x 18" batting
- ½ yd. fusible web
- Appliqué materials for corresponding flowers:

  Red Flower: 8" x 8" red; 8" x 8" green; 8" x 8" dark green; scrap of dark red

  Pink Flower: 8" x 8" pale pink or pale yellow; scraps of medium pink, dark pink and speckled medium pink

  Yellow Flower: 8" x 8" yellow dot fabric; 8" x 8" different yellow dot fabric; scrap of dark yellow; 18" of yarn or thick thread for stamens
- Decorative threads for embellishing, detailing and quilting
- Temporary spray adhesive (optional)
- Appliqué patterns in back of book: Flower 1, Flower 2, or Flower 3
- General sewing tools (Chapter 1)

Note: The flower patterns are available in two sizes. This project is made using the larger-size flower appliqués.

Construction and Quilting

1. Refer to the Precious Petals Trilogy Layout Diagram to position each piece of your wall hanging.

2. Use an accurate ¼" seam to sew the following: A + B; AB + C; ABC + D, ABCD + E. Press the seams toward the outer border. Square up after each border is added.

3. Trace and cut out each element of your flower, following the fusible web manufacturer's directions. Trace the larger-size flower appliqués.

4. Create a flower appliqué unit using a nonstick pressing sheet as described in Chapter 1. Refer to the coordinating Flower Layout Diagram to position the parts as you make this unit. Note that the Flower 1 pieces 1 and 1A are labeled in the same leaf; align those labels and let 1A peek out from underneath, as shown in the photos.

5. Fuse the flower unit to the pieced background. Finish the raw edges as you prefer.

6. Baste, quilt, embellish and bind the piece as desired. Consider using temporary spray adhesive to baste your wall hanging, which will save you time and effort.

7. Add a hanging sleeve and label.

Tip

The flower patterns resemble several common varieties. Change the flower colors to adapt them to fit your local favorites. Add detail to each flower with machine thread work, hand embroidery, beads, couched yarns, sequins or other embellishments. Position the flower units at different angles, if you prefer. Try different color ways to get the perfect look for your décor.

Precious Petals Wall Hanging

Cut

From	Size	How Many	For
A	6½" square	3	Background
B	1½" x 6½"	6	Inner border
C	1½" x 8½"	6	Inner border
D	2½" x 8½"	2	Outer border
E	3½" x 8½"	2	Outer border
F	3½" x 34½"	2	Outer border
Binding fabric	2½"-wide strips	3	Binding

Finished size: 14" x 34".

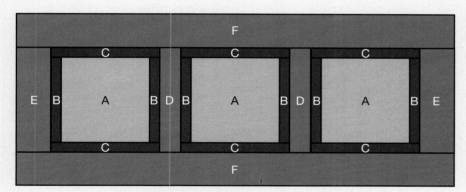

Precious Petals Wall Hanging Layout Diagram

You Will Need

- ⅝ yd. dark print (outer border, binding)
- ¼ yd. dark solid (inner border)
- ¼ yd. light print (background)
- ⅝ yd. coordinating fabric (quilt back, hanging sleeve)
- ½ yd. batting
- 1 yd. fusible web
- Appliqué materials for corresponding flowers:

  Red Flower: 6" x 6" red; 6" x 6" green; 6" x 6" dark green; scrap of dark red

  Pink Flower: 6" x 6" pale pink or pale yellow; scraps of medium pink, dark pink and speckled medium pink

  Yellow Flower: 6" x 6" yellow dot fabric; 6" x 6" different yellow dot fabric; scrap of dark yellow; 18" of yarn or thick thread for stamens
- Decorative threads for sewing, embellishing, detailing and quilting
- Appliqué patterns:
  Small Flower 1, Small Flower 2, Small Flower 3
- General sewing tools (Chapter 1)

Note: Flower patterns are shown in two sizes. This project is made with the smaller-size flower appliqués.

Construction & Quilting

1. Refer to the Precious Petals Wall Hanging Layout Diagram to position each piece of your wall hanging.

2. Sew with accurate ¼" seam in alphabetical order: A + B; AB + C. Press the seams toward the outer border. Square up each framed background unit to measure 8½" square. Repeat to make three units total.

3. Add D and E pieces as shown to create a row. Press the seams toward the outer borders.

4. Add F pieces. Press the seams toward the outer borders.

5. Continue with the directions given for the Precious Petals Trilogy Wall Hangings, beginning with Step 3. You will be working with a smaller version of each flower; refer to the Small Flower Layout Diagrams as you make each unit.

6. Baste, quilt, embellish and bind the piece as desired.

7. Add a hanging sleeve and label.

Glossary

Just as languages evolve and meanings change, so do phrases and terms in quilting. Here are explanations of specific words and phrases used in this book.

Appliqué design unit — A fusible web design, such as a flower or goose, made of many intricate parts that have been fused together into a single movable appliqué design. See also Nonstick pressing sheet.

Audition fabric — To lay out the fabrics chosen for a project to see if the combination is effective. This often is done by overlapping fabrics, with more fabric showing for pieces that will be used in larger sizes than others. Auditioning also is done to select border fabrics and to determine appropriate border widths.

Bias — Fabric grain at a 45-degree angle to the selvage. Fabric is weakest along the bias; it allows the most stretch and is easily distorted. Fabric cut on the bias often is used in conjunction with curves.

Checkerboard strip — Alternating colored squares sewn together to form a length that is one square tall x any number of squares long.

Cross-cut — To cut across one or more seams of a strata unit, often forming a portion of a block or border. This also can pertain to cutting strips of fabric into smaller pieces.

Cross grain of fabric — The grain that is perpendicular the selvage. The cross grain allows some stretch, but it can be distorted. Strips and borders used for quilting often are cut on the cross grain (selvage to selvage) for economy of fabric.

Design wall — A flat surface covered with punch fleece, batting or flannel that allows fabric placement without pinning. Quilters easily can arrange and rearrange blocks or pieces of a project on a design wall, and they can visualize sewn blocks or projects before any actual sewing is done. The phrase "work surface" is used interchangeably.

Easing — Evenly working in excess fabric as you sew, matching the length of a longer unit with a shorter one. This often is done with borders or when sewing two blocks of similar but unequal size.

Finished size — The size of a block or unit after all seams have been sewn. The calculated finished size doesn't necessarily match the sewn finished size. See also Square up.

Freezer paper — A white, coated paper sold in rolls at grocery stores that can be used as a pattern or as a removable stabilizer. The paper side is the dull side; the shiny side is waxy and can be ironed to fabric using a dry iron. Freezer paper leaves no residue on fabric when it is removed, and it can be reused several times.

Fusible or fusible web — A flat, dry, glue product used to adhere fabrics together, often with paper on one or both sides and glue substance on the other. Fusible web most often is ironed to fabric, and it is used in fusible appliqués. Several varieties of fusible web are available, each with unique characteristics.

Fussy cut — To cut a required size and shape, but to specifically center a design of the fabric in that shape. This technique often is used with novelty prints or large motifs. Consider the grain of fabric when fussy cutting.

Grain of fabric — The direction or arrangement of fibers in fabric. See also Straight of grain, Bias and Cross grain of fabric.

Layout diagram — A drawing that shows where to place all of the pieces of a wall hanging. In relation to fusible web appliqué, the drawing refers to the placement of all of the small parts that make up a design, like a flower, goose or fishing creel. The diagram is used as a guide to overlap pieces as they are placed onto a background fabric or fused into a larger unit using a pressing sheet.

Nonstick pressing sheet — A flexible sheet product, often made of Teflon, that is able to withstand heat without melting or distorting. The pressing sheet can be used as a protective layer above or below fabric. Fabric pieces with fusible web on them can be ironed to the sheet in layers, cooled in place and then peeled off intact as a single appliqué design unit.

Satin stitch — A very close, machine zigzag stitch. The width used will vary by project. Begin with a standard zigzag stitch and gradually shorten the stitch length; if stitching starts bunching up on top of itself, lengthen the stitch slightly.

Scant — A bit less than the size given; for example, a scant ¼" seam measures about ³⁄₁₆" wide.

Segment — A portion cut from a larger piece or strip.

Selvage — The tightly woven outer edges of fabric, often with brand names and color dots printed on them. The selvage seldom is used in projects because it handles differently than the rest of the fabric.

Speedy triangles — Also known as Fast Corner Triangles, Quick Corners or Connector Squares. This method is used to add a triangle to another piece of fabric. See Chapter 1 for the actual process.

Square up — To verify and make corrections to a block or smaller unit so the actual sewn size is the same as the calculated size. Adjustments may need to be made in seam width or pressing.

Stabilizer — A product added below a base fabric to keep it from bunching up when stitched, such as when raw edges of a fused design are zigzag stitched; stitching goes through all layers. Stabilizer can be removable (paper or tear-away products), or it can become part of the finished piece.

Stay stitch — A line of stitching sewn to stabilize the edge of fabric or to keep seams from opening up with handling. A stay stitch usually is sewn a little narrower than whatever the seam width would be, and it follows a normal stitch length. Stay stitches generally are not seen in a finished item.

Straight of grain — The fabric grain that runs parallel to the selvage. Fabric on the straight of grain is strongest and allows the least amount of stretch. Borders often are cut on the straight of grain for stability, but they also require more yardage.

Strata — Two or more strips of fabric of varying widths and lengths sewn together to form a larger piece of fabric.

Strip — A strip of fabric cut on the cross grain, most often cut from selvage to selvage, to make a piece that is the width specified and approximately 40" to 44" long.

Topstitch — To sew a line of stitching near a finished edge. Topstitching usually is a bit longer than the normal stitch length; it also is visible in a finished item.

Unfinished size — The size of a block or unit before all of the outer seams are sewn. The calculated unfinished size doesn't necessarily match the sewn unfinished size.

Whipstitch — To sew two layers of fabric together by hand, often when finishing a pillow after inserting a pillow form.

Contributors

Here's a handy list of resources to help you on your quilting journey. Check your local quilt shop for the fabrics, threads, rulers and other supplies used to make these projects. Information listings were correct at the time of publication.

Ackfeld Manufacturing

Manufacturer of quilt hangers; provided those featured with Freedom's Flight Wall Hanging and Fish-In-A-Round Wall Hanging
P.O. Box 539
Reeds Spring, MO 65737
Phone: (888) 272-3135
Fax: (417) 272-3160
E-mail: admin@ackfeldwire.com
Web: www.ackfeldwire.com

Bernina of America Inc.

Manufacturer of sewing machines
3702 Prairie Lake Court
Aurora, IL 60504
Phone: (630) 978-2500
Web: www.berninausa.com

Golden Eagle Log Homes

Manufacturer of quality log homes; provided log home locations used for photo shoots in this book
4421 Plover Road
Wisconsin Rapids, WI 54494
Phone: (800) 270-5025
Fax: (715) 421-2002
E-mail: goldnegl@wctc.net
Web: www.goldeneagleloghomes.com

Krause Publications

Publisher of this and other quality how-to books for quilting, sewing and other crafts
700 E. State St.
Iola, WI 54990-0001
Phone: (888) 457-2873
Web: www.krause.com

Machine Quilting by Dawn Kelly

Machine quilting for Northern Exposure Throw
160 McNearney Road
Ponderay, ID 83852
Phone: (208) 263-7075
E-mail: dkelly@televar.com

Moose Country Quilts

Featuring patterns, classes and catalogs by author Terrie Kralik
P.O. Box 902
Bonners Ferry, ID 83805
Phone: (208) 267-0713
E-mail: moosequilts@hotmail.com
Web: www.moosecountryquilts.com

P&B Textiles

Manufacturer of fabrics to inspire you, including fabrics used for several projects in this book
Web: www.pbtex.com

Splendid Stitches

Machine quilting by Aimee Simmons on Bear's Paw Quilt
Phone: (208) 265-7888
E-mail: aimee@splendidstitches.com
Web: www.splendidstitches.com

Sulky of America, Inc.

Manufacturer of threads, stabilizers and spray adhesives used for projects in this book
Phone: (800) 874-4115 (to obtain a mail-order source)
Web: www.sulky.com

The Warm Company

Manufacturer of Warm & Natural batting and Steam-A-Seam fusible web
954 East Union St.
Seattle, WA 98122
Phone: (800) 234-9276
Web: www.warmcompany.com

Timber Lane Press

Timtex stiff interfacing is made exclusively for this company, which will take wholesale orders or recommend retail outlets
24350 N. Rimrock Road
Hayden, ID 83835
Phone: (208) 765-3353
E-mail: qltblox@earthlink.net

Resources

Annie's Attic

1 Annie Lane
Big Sandy, TX 75755
Phone: (800) 582-6643
Web: www.anniesattic.com

Clotilde LLC

P.O. Box 7500
Big Sandy, TX 75755-7500
Phone: (800) 772-2891
Web: www.clotilde.com

Connecting Threads

P.O. Box 870760
Vancouver, WA 98687-7760
Phone: (800) 574-6454
Web: www.ConnectingThreads.com

Home Sew

P.O. Box 4099
Bethlehem, PA 18018-0099
Phone: (800) 344-4739
Web: www.homesew.com

Keepsake Quilting

Route 25
P.O. Box 1618
Center Harbor, NH 03226-1618
Phone: (800) 438-5464
Web: www.keepsakequilting.com

Martingale & Co.

Manufacturer of Bias Square Ruler
20205 144th Ave. NE
Woodinville, WA 98072-8478
Phone: (800) 426-3126
Web: www.martingale-pub.com

Nancy's Notions

333 Beichl Ave.
PO Box 683
Beaver Dam, WI 53916-0683
Phone: (800) 833-0690
Web: www.nancysnotions.com

Olfa-North America

Manufacturer of rotary cutters and mats
33 S. Sixth St.
Terre Haute, IN 47807
Phone: (800) 962-6532
Web: www.olfarotary.com

favorite CLASSICS

**22 Favorite Pieces for
Early Intermediate through
Late Intermediate Students
from the Four Stylistic Periods
of Piano Repertoire**

SOLO BOOK ONE

Selected & Edited by E. L. Lancaster & Kenon D. Renfrow

About This Collection

The 22 pieces in this collection have proven to be favorites of early intermediate through late intermediate students throughout the years. Chosen from the four stylistic periods of piano repertoire, the volume contains selections of varying difficulty levels so that it may be used over a two- to three-year period.

A companion volume, *Favorite Classics— Accompaniment Book One* (Alfred #6024), contains specially composed second keyboard parts for the teacher, parent or a more advanced student. The pieces in each collection have a page-by-page cross reference, and measures are numbered to facilitate ease of use. The second keyboard part may be played on a second piano or electronic instrument and may be recorded or sequenced to enhance practice, learning and performance.

A General MIDI disk (Alfred #14425), available separately, contains accompaniments for each piece in the collection. Accompaniments were especially created to enhance the musical performance in a stylistic manner. The accompaniments on the disk were recorded on separate tracks allowing teachers to use only those tracks needed for study, practice or performance. The right hand and left hand of each piece as well as the orchestrated accompaniments and rhythm parts were recorded on separate tracks.

An icon shows the TRACK number for each example on the General MIDI disk: **1 (25)** The first number after the icon is the TRACK number for the Type 0 MIDI file; the second number (in parentheses) is the TRACK number of the Type 1 MIDI file.

Second Edition
Copyright © MCMXCVIII by Alfred Publishing Co., Inc.
All rights reserved. Printed in USA.

Cover Design: Jane Wong
Art Direction: Ted Engelbart

Front Cover: clockwise from upper right; Johann Sebastian Bach, Leopold Mozart, Carl Maria von Weber and Aram Khachaturian.

Alfred

SUGGESTED ORDER OF STUDY

The following is a suggested order of study for early intermediate through late intermediate levels. Students should study pieces from the various style periods simultaneously.

CONTENTS

Rondino

Use with
FAVORITE CLASSICS
Accompaniment Book One,
page 3.

Jean-Philippe Rameau
(1683-1764)

Minuet

K. 73b; L. 217

Domenico Scarlatti
(1685-1757)

Use with
FAVORITE CLASSICS
Accompaniment Book One,
page 4.

2 (26)

Moderato

Use with
FAVORITE CLASSICS
Accompaniment Book One,
page 6.

Menuet in G Major

from the *Notebook for Anna Magdalena*

🔊 **3 (27)**

Johann Sebastian Bach
(1685-1750)

Allegro moderato

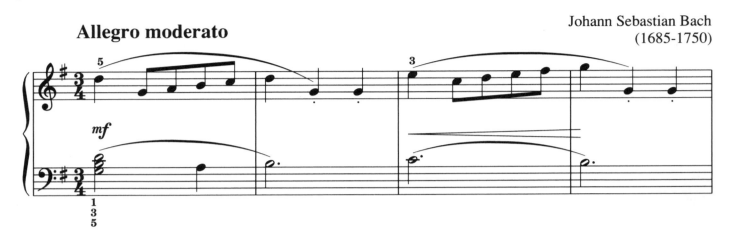

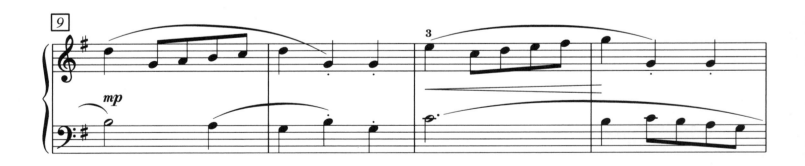

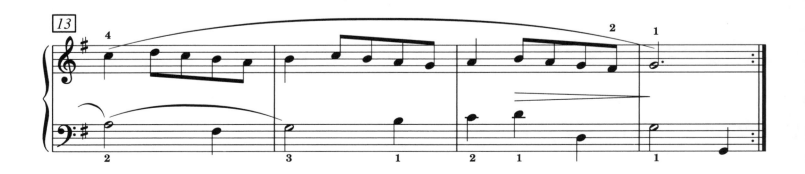

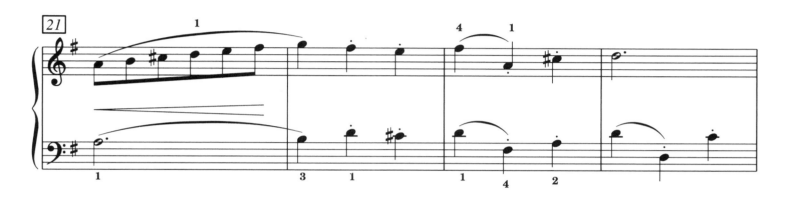

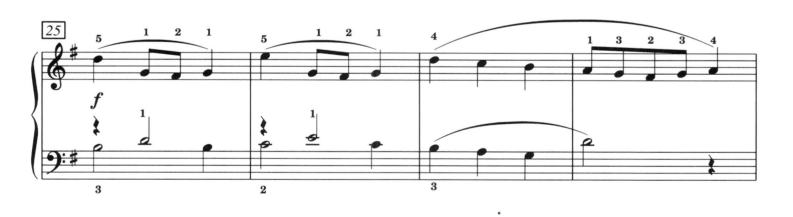

Use with
FAVORITE CLASSICS
Accompaniment Book One,
page 8.

Menuet in G Minor
from the *Notebook for Anna Magdalena*

Johann Sebastian Bach
(1685-1750)

🔊 4 (28)

Moderato

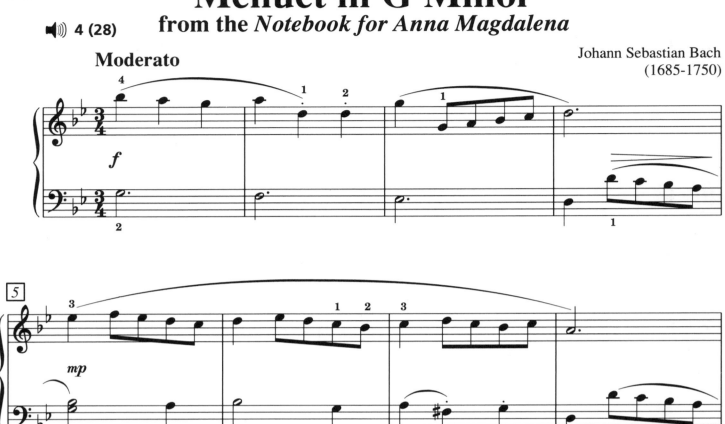

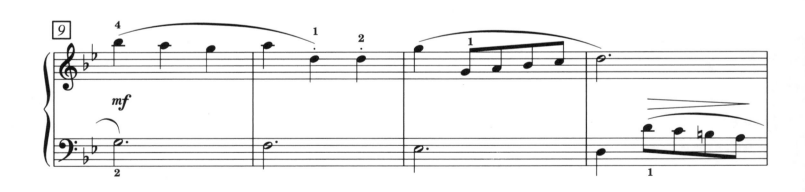

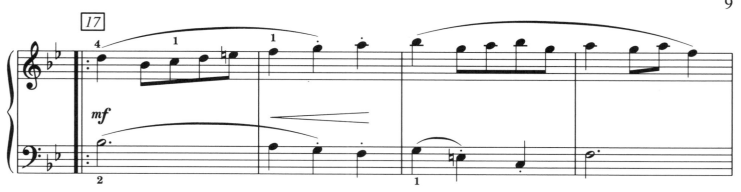

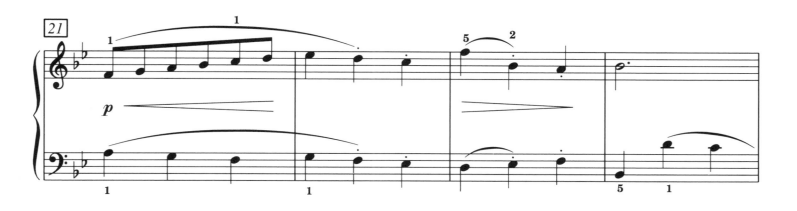

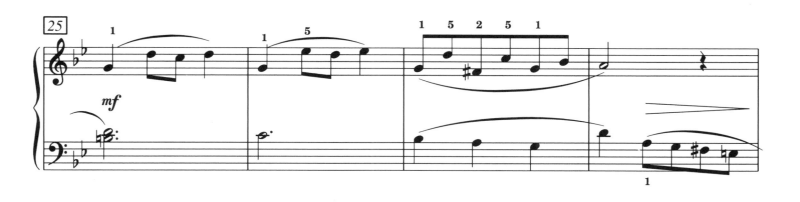

Use with
FAVORITE CLASSICS
Accompaniment Book One,
page 10.

Musette in D Major
from the *Notebook for Anna Magdalena*

5 (29)

Johann Sebastian Bach
(1685-1750)

Moderato

Ecossaise
WoO 23

Use with
FAVORITE CLASSICS
Accompaniment Book One,
page 14.

Ludwig van Beethoven
(1770-1827)

🔊 **6 (30)**

Allegro

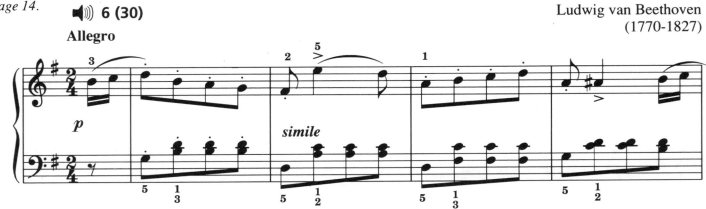

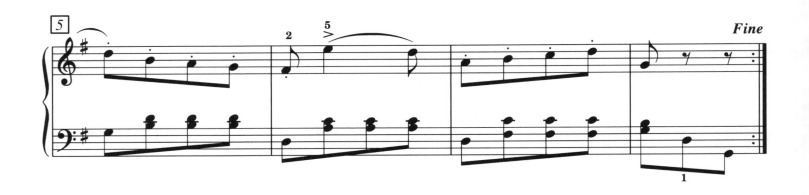

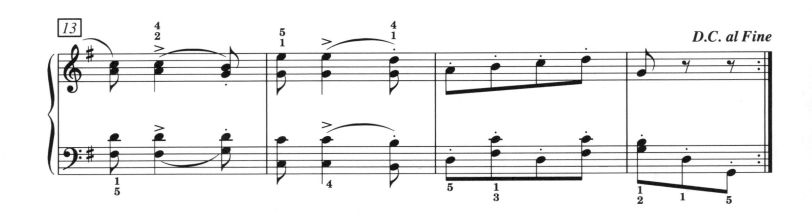

Use with
FAVORITE CLASSICS
Accompaniment Book One,
page 12.

Bagatelle in A Minor
Op. 119, No. 9

Ludwig van Beethoven
(1770-1827)

7 (31)

Vivace moderato

Use with
FAVORITE CLASSICS
Accompaniment Book One,
page 16.

Bagatelle
Op. 125, No. 10

Anton Diabelli
(1781-1858)

🔊 **8 (32)**

Allegretto

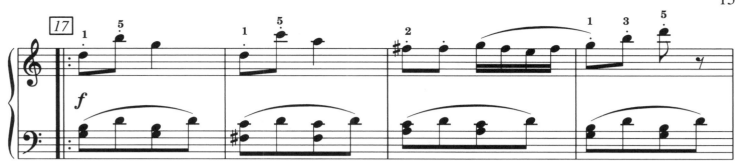

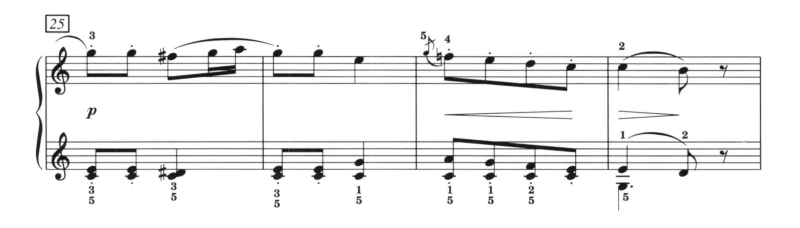

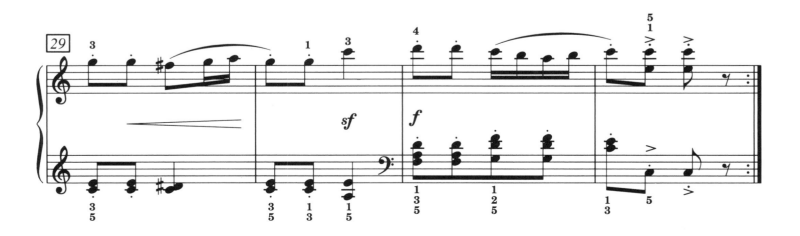

Use with
FAVORITE CLASSICS
Accompaniment Book One,
page 18.

Solfeggio in C Minor

Carl Philipp Emanuel Bach
(1714-1788)

Presto 🔊 **9 (33)**

Use with
FAVORITE CLASSICS
Accompaniment Book One,
page 15.

Burleske
from *Notebook for Wolfgang*

Leopold Mozart
(1719-1787)

🔊 **10 (34)**

Allegro

LH detached

Use with
FAVORITE CLASSICS
Accompaniment Book One,
page 24.

Sonatina in C Major
Op. 36, No. 1

Muzio Clementi
(1752–1832)

Use with
FAVORITE CLASSICS
Accompaniment Book One,
page 27.

🔊 **12 (36)**

Andante

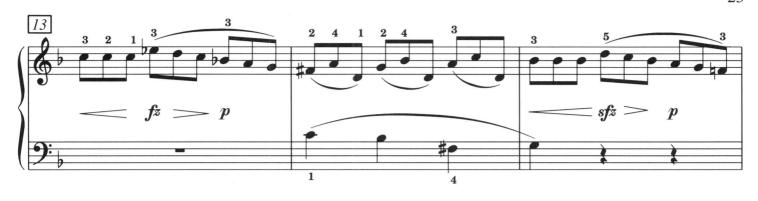

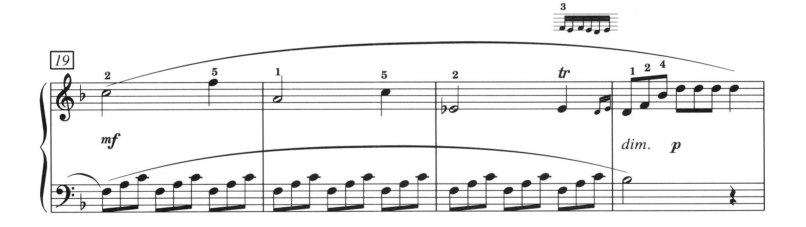

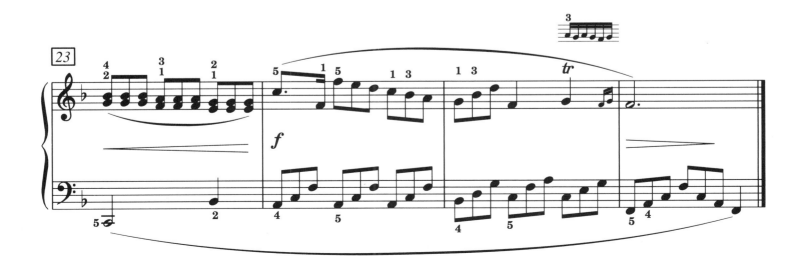

Use with
FAVORITE CLASSICS
Accompaniment Book One,
page 29.

🔊 **13 (37)**

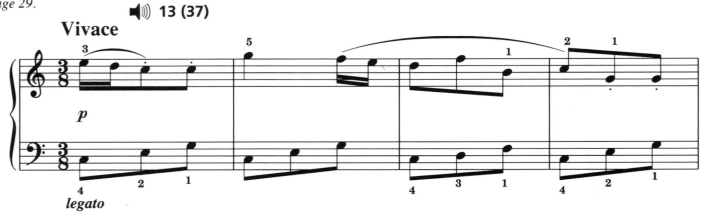

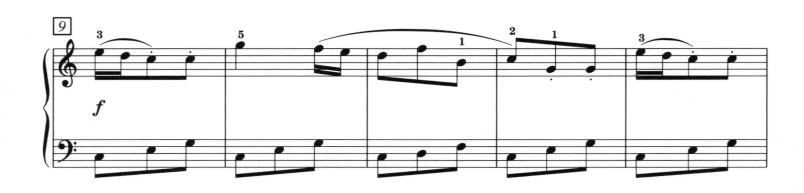

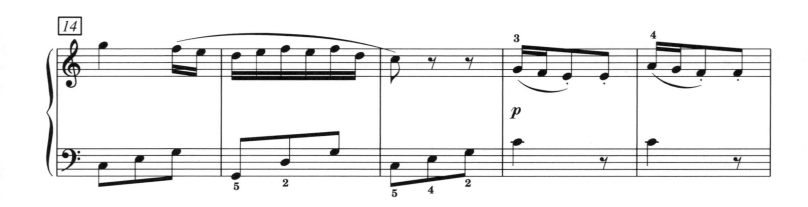

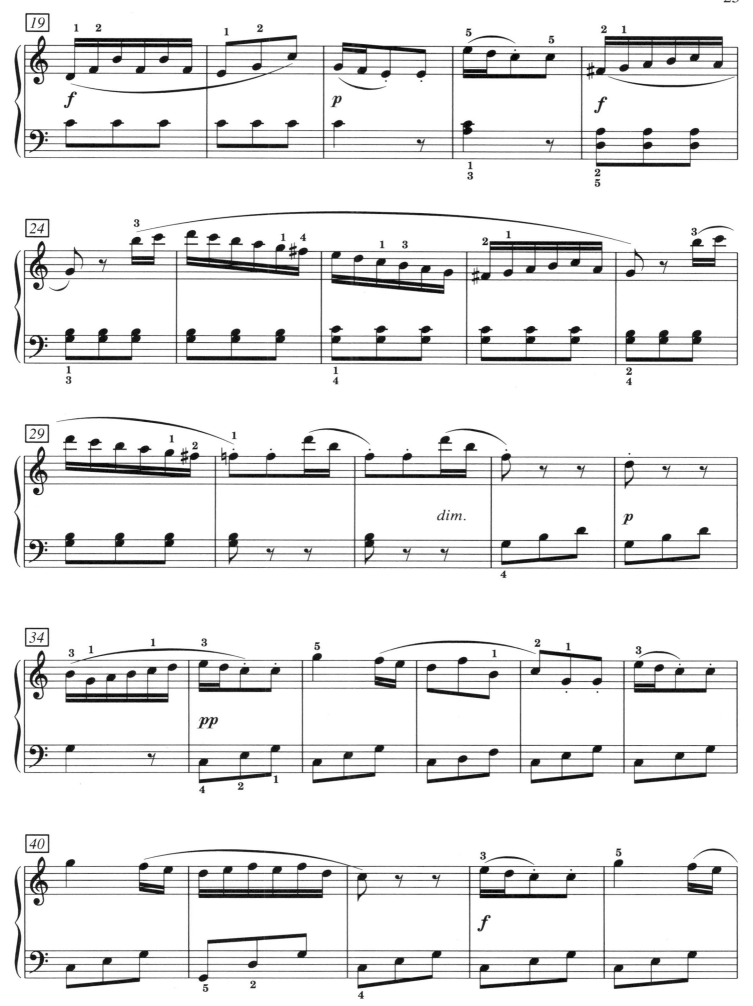

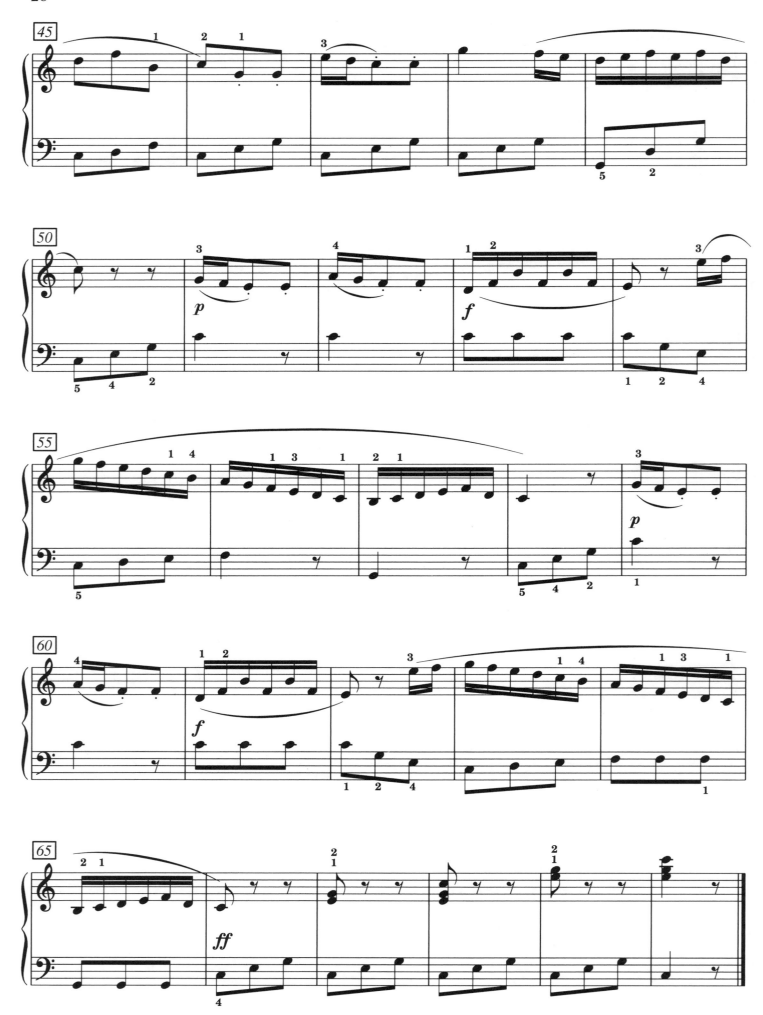

Melody
Op. 68, No. 1

Robert Schumann
(1810-1856)

Use with
FAVORITE CLASSICS
Accompaniment Book One,
page 40.

14 (38)

Moderato

Use with
FAVORITE CLASSICS
Accompaniment Book One,
page 38.

Arabesque
Op. 100, No. 2

Johann Burgmüller
(1806-1874)

🔊 **15 (39)**

Allegro scherzando

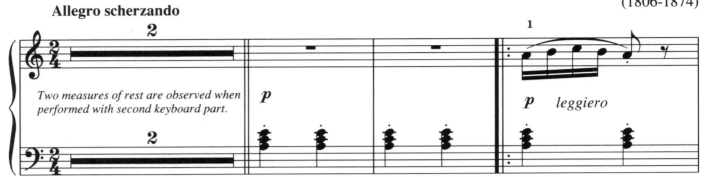

Two measures of rest are observed when
performed with second keyboard part.

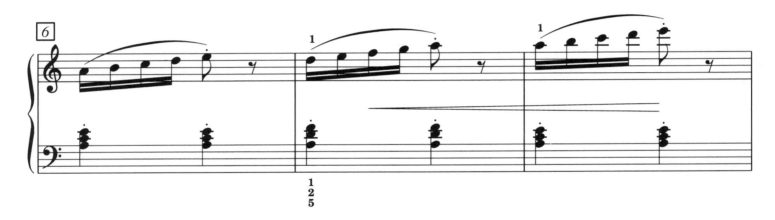

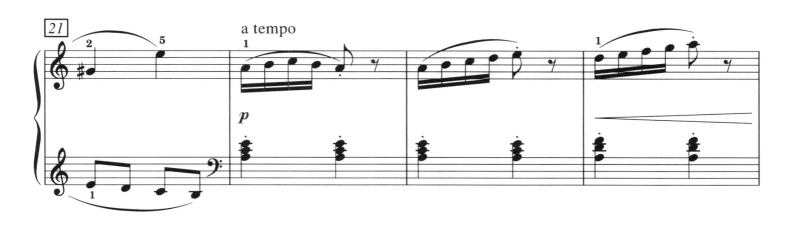

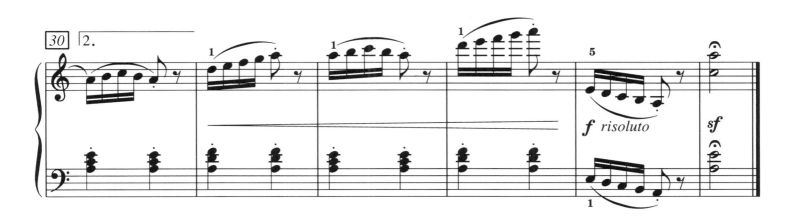

Ballade
Op. 100, No. 15

Use with
FAVORITE CLASSICS
Accompaniment Book One,
page 33.

Johann Burgmüller
(1806-1874)

🔊 **16 (40)**

Two measures of rest are observed when performed with second keyboard part.

Use with
FAVORITE CLASSICS
Accompaniment Book One,
page 46.

The Avalanche
Op. 45, No. 2

Stephen Heller
(1813-1888)

🔊 **17 (41)**

Allegro vivace

poco meno mosso

a tempo

Use with
FAVORITE CLASSICS
Accompaniment Book One,
page 42.

The Wild Rider
Op. 68, No. 8

Robert Schumann
(1810-1856)

🔊 **18 (42)**

Allegro

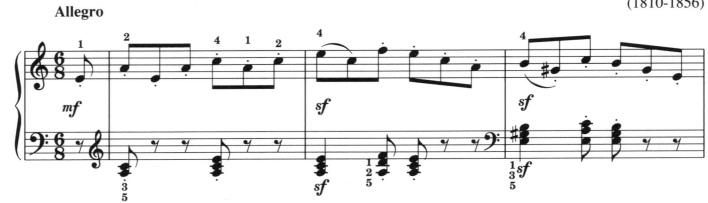

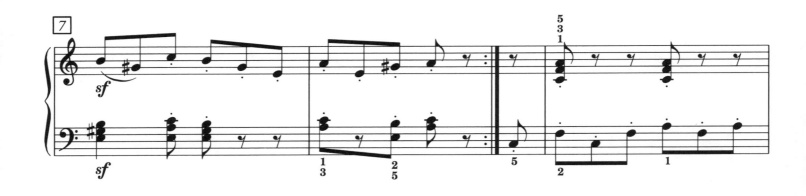

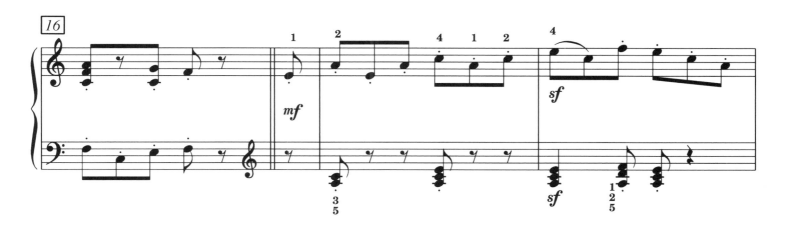

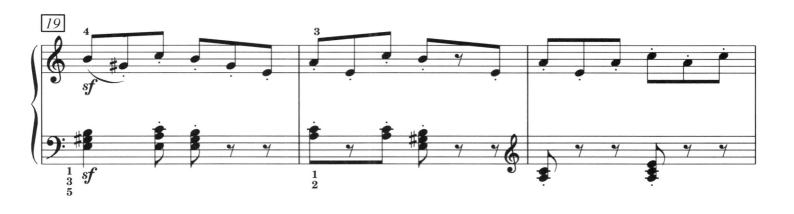

Scherzo

Use with
FAVORITE CLASSICS
Accompaniment Book One,
page 44.

Carl Maria von Weber
(1786-1826)

🔊 **19 (43)**

Allegretto

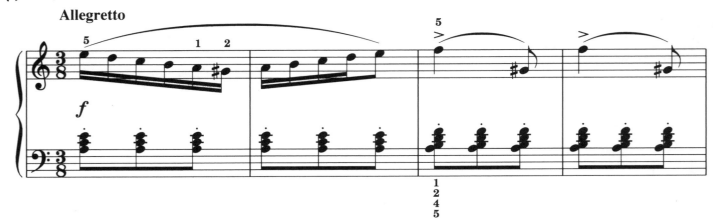

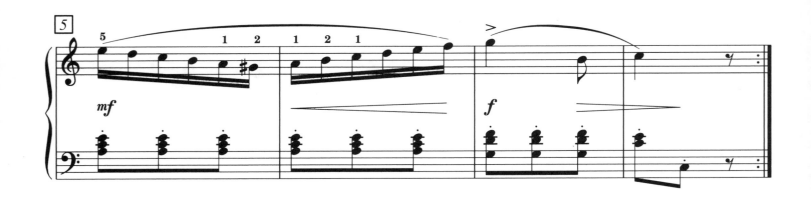

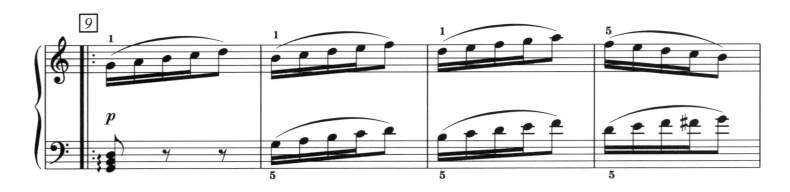

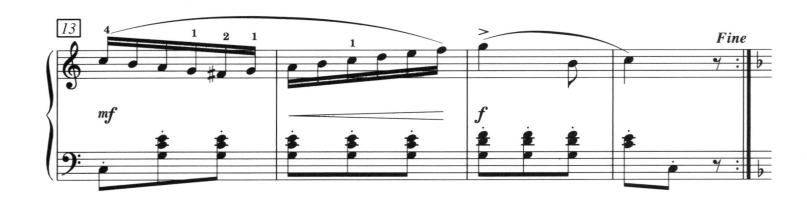

Spinning Song
Op. 14, No. 4

Use with
FAVORITE CLASSICS
Accompaniment Book One,
page 51.

Albert Ellmenreich
(1816-1905)

🔊 20 (44)

Allegretto

Galop
Op. 39, No. 18

Use with
FAVORITE CLASSICS
Accompaniment Book One,
page 56.

Dmitri Kabalevsky
(1904-1987)

21 (45)

Use with
FAVORITE CLASSICS
Accompaniment Book One,
page 58.

Ivan Sings

Aram Khachaturian
(1903-1978)

22 (46)

Andantino

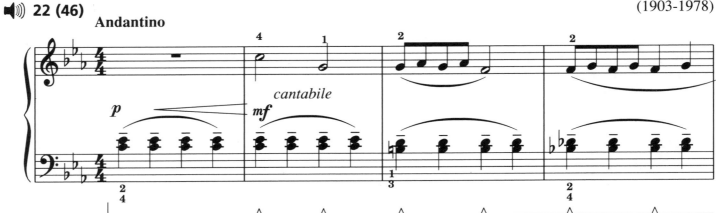

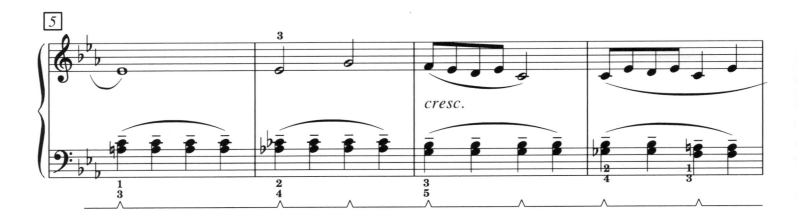

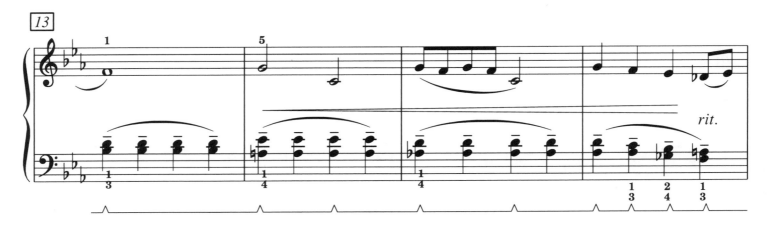

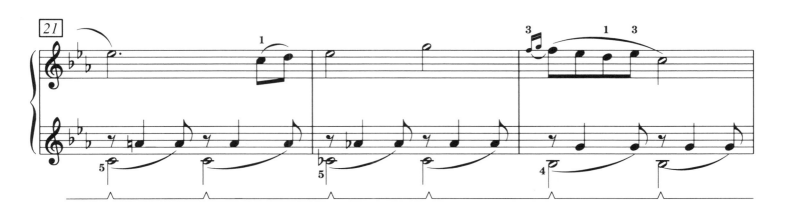

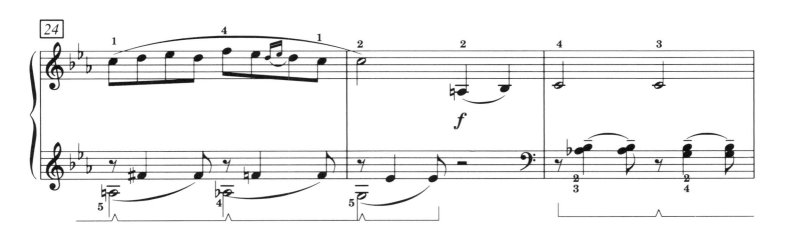

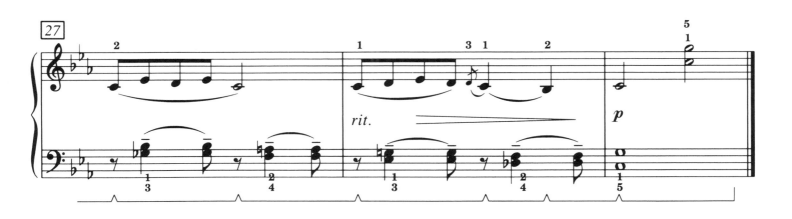

Use with
FAVORITE CLASSICS
Accompaniment Book One,
page 61.

Toccatina
Op. 27, No. 12

Dmitri Kabalevsky
(1904-1987)

Use with
FAVORITE CLASSICS
Accompaniment Book One,
page 64.

Clowns
Op. 39, No. 20

Dmitri Kabalevsky
(1904-1987)

🔊 **24 (48)**

Allegro

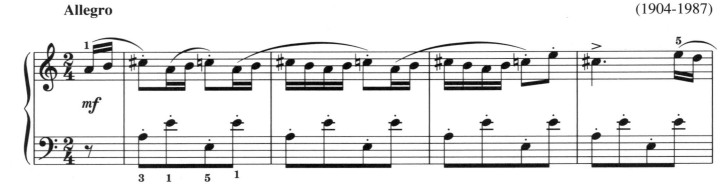

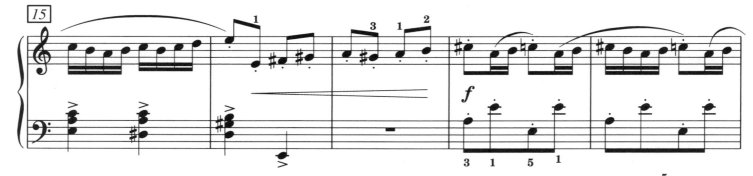

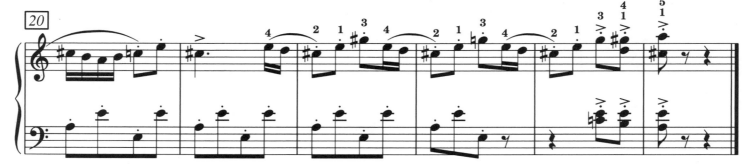